Imaginative
POTTERY

Imaginative POTTERY

David Harvey

A & C Black · London

Second edition 1983
A & C Black (Publishers) Ltd, 35 Bedford Row,
London WC1R 4JH

First published 1976 by Pitman Publishing Ltd

ISBN 0-7136-2380-2

Printed in Great Britain at
The Pitman Press, Bath

Contents

Introduction

Clay is a very abundant material in all parts of the world. It is seldom necessary to venture far in order to discover a readily available source. As a child, living in the suburbs of London, I remember that we discovered beautifully plastic clay right in our own back garden when we excavated the footings for our air-raid shelter. My sister and I passed many happy hours making all manner of objects with this clay. We used it with grass and twigs to make model native villages. It was shaped into fierce beasts from the jungle, warriors, cattle, totem-poles and sacrificial offerings which could be put to death in all manner of terrible ways. It made the essential ingredient of the most mouth-watering banquets: roast turkey with peas and potatoes, a boar's head on a charger—with a lemon stuck in its mouth, bananas, pears, grapes, sliced watermelon and many other items which in times of food rationing never appeared on any other table.

On Hallowe'en night we made the most grotesque face masks from clay. Large staring eye sockets and hideously gaping mouths were carved through the clay, and eyeballs and tombstone-like teeth were stood into the appropriate apertures. As darkness came we illuminated the masks with candles and provoked each other into flights of outrageous imagination about witches, demons and spells. We reassured ourselves that we had nothing to fear because we were protected from harm by the clay charms which hung around our necks. That night we vented all our spite on the miserable old lady who lived next door. We thought we would finally put an end to her complaints and her clay effigy was transfixed with pins in all manner of places. We were only mildly surprised to see her appear the next day with a bandaged hand!

Our deepest fears of war, bombs and sudden death were given emotional outlets in our play with clay, and with continued experience we became more skilled and more ambitious in our projects. We made zoos, an ark, grottoes, wedding sets and we even had our own court trial of clay characters. We made

1

and decorated some clay vessels and tried to fire them in the bonfire, but they blew up. We never understood why and there was no expert potter to come to our rescue. We had no help from school either because in those days the plastic arts only went as far as plasticine, otherwise we might have progressed to more sophisticated methods and processes.

As children, however, we were fortunate to have free access to an enticing material which fully satisfied some of our basic human needs. It was a means of making our statements in our own way. It exercised our imagination to the full and developed our manipulative talents. It provided us with an outlet for our emotions and a challenge to our inventiveness. Times have changed since those days but human needs have not—unless the needs are greater now than ever in the often sterile times of the motor car, high-rise flats and the TV set. It is a sobering thought that some of our children seldom, if ever, see an open fire today. The privileged childhood experience we enjoyed should be the right of everyone.

The urge to create is latent in all of us. It is a very vital part of our lives which we cannot afford to neglect. For the very young child clay is a material to be squeezed, poked, squashed, rolled, torn apart and thumped together again. Through this opportunity of exploration the child will be launched on an exciting voyage of discovery. Manipulative skills will gradually emerge which will enable clay to be used as a means of making images and communicating ideas, thus stimulating imagination and invention. Age and experience will bring their measure of sophistication to the activity but the pleasure and satisfaction, through all levels of development, can be very rewarding. There is no upper or lower age limit for those interested in experimenting with clay. There are no absolute standards to be aimed at. The voyage of discovery is con-tinuous. The methods and processes defined here are only signposts pointing along the way and will assume less importance as the reader gradually finds his own direction. Critical observation, free play of imagination and inventiveness will make the journey more varied and interesting. Along the route we will, from time to time, be concerned with aspects of interest to the archaeologist, historian and geologist, the chemist, the physicist, the mathematician and even the musician as well as to the artist and craftsman who wants to design, draw, paint and work in three-dimensional form.

There is no need to spend much money on expensive apparatus and equip-ment. Some of the kilns described can be made at no cost, other than the labour involved, if you have access to local clay and second-hand bricks. A strong, fine sieve for preparing clay and glazes is likely to be the most expensive item you will need. Most other items, such as plastic detergent bottles, buckets, forks, knives, rolling-pins, etc. can be borrowed from the kitchen.

It is quite likely that you will be able to collect your own local clay from the garden, a building site or road works and you can make your own pigments from ground rust and Bordeaux mixture (a tomato fungicide). Glazes can be prepared from finely crushed bottles or broken windscreen glass found in most motorway lay-bys. The local joiner or carpenter may let you have sawdust, shavings and wood offcuts to fire your pots with. In the book a wide range of shaping and decorating processes will be explored and a variety of kilns and firing methods that can be used in schools or in the back garden at home will be considered. There are also some answers to the problems of pottery for the flat-dweller. The processes, whilst primarily directed to the enthusiastic amateur, will also be found to contain items of interest to the more experienced potter.

Not everyone will have the opportunity to build an oil-fired stoneware kiln for reduction firings, but once you get involved with pottery you will find it very compelling and difficult to curtail your enthusiasm; your question 'how do I start?' will become 'how do I stop?'

1 Starting with fire and clay

The softness of damp clay and its dried strength have favoured the use of clay as a constructional material for thousands of years. Swallows, nuthatches and thrushes use clay in the construction of their nests and termite colonies have built clay mounds of astonishing proportions. There is some evidence even in Upper Paleolithic times (12 000–10 000 B.C.), when primitive man was hunting mammoths with weapons made of stone, that he built simple shelters constructed with mud and turf. Certainly by late Mesolithic times (5000–4000 B.C.) he was building houses with compacted clay walls such as those discovered at Jarmo on the foothills east of the Tigris. In addition to shelter, primitive man had need of fire for warmth and it is not surprising that the effect of heat on clay was soon recognized and deliberately put to use. Fire-hardened clay models of animals were produced during the last Ice Age at Vestonice in Moravia. In course of time man discovered more efficient ways of using heat to make stronger vessels for domestic use and ritual ceremony.

Discovering and identifying clay

Because it was difficult to transport heavy materials over long distances it was necessary to use local resources. The fires were fed with wood or other available fuel collected from the locality. The original sources of clay which prehistoric man used are probably still in existence today. Even where early settlements of man have grown into the large towns and cities of today we can often see evidence of the clay beds which were perhaps used by the early settlers.

As the foundations for new buildings are excavated, as new drainage systems are laid down, as roadways are constructed through town and country, fine examples of rich plastic clays will often be revealed as they are carved

Fig. 1   House Martin at her nest which is built mainly with clay and grass straw

Fig 2   Collecting clay from a motorway site

out by excavators and disposed of by dumper trucks and lorries. A polite request to the builders is all that it will probably cost to secure as much clay as you can carry away with you. Although you will have to be content with the specific qualities of clays which may thus become available, you will gain a much fuller understanding of their nature by preparing and using such materials. Architects, surveyors, builders, farm workers, miners, gardeners and various other earthworkers will often be able to advise you about local clay deposits. Disused brick-clay pits may be marked on old maps. Geological maps are helpful to a point, but they define the gross soil structures without specifying the overlying surface deposits which may make it awkward or impossible to reach usable clay. Nor will they give account of localized, easily reached, pockets of good clay.

It is the stickiness or plasticity of clay which makes it easy to recognize and there is a very simple test for plasticity which can be easily carried out on the spot. If the sample of clay has been freshly dug up it will usually be fairly damp and soft enough to shape into a thin roll which can then be wrapped round the finger. The results may be interpreted as follows:

Sample 1. Sample will not hold together to form a roll—this is not clay.
Sample 2. Roll breaks when wrapped round finger—very low clay content.
Sample 3. Deep cracks in roll when bent round finger—a coarse, gritty, low-plasticity clay. (A 'short' clay.)
Sample 4. Small, shallow cracks in roll when bent round—a good, useful, plastic clay.
Sample 5. Roll bends easily and preserves a shiny, unbroken surface—a fine-grained, highly plastic clay. (A 'fat' clay.)

Fig. 3 Finger ring tests: (1) loamy earth; (2) very low clay content; (3) coarse, gritty, low-plasticity clay; (4) a good, useful plastic clay; (5) fine-grained, highly plastic clay

The clay sample should be taken from an adequate depth to avoid contamination with surface soil. If stones or gravel occur in the clay this could make preparation tedious and it may be better to find a purer source of supply. Certainly clay is a very common material which is not usually difficult to find. Once you have identified your clay sample by the 'finger ring' test you will be able to decide whether it is suitable for your purpose. If you want clay to use only for modelling purposes and have no intention of firing (baking) it, the ring test is the only one you need make to see if the clay is sufficiently plastic for this use. Very short clays will crumble too easily whereas very fat clays will be too sticky, they will shrink too much and probably crack as they dry out. A clay somewhere between these two extremes is best for modelling. If very fat and very short clays are available they can be mixed together in proportions which will produce the desired characteristics, or a very fat clay can be mixed with fine sand to make a good modelling clay. Sand used in this way is called an 'opener' because it opens the texture of the clay and creates rather more generous passageways between the clay particles through which moisture can escape rapidly; drying will be more even throughout. Uneven drying will produce uneven shrinkage which will result in stresses which may split the clay shape.

Freshly dug clay will often be sufficiently moist to use directly, but it must be understood that because the clay is damper than the surrounding atmosphere there will be a loss of water from the clay to the atmosphere which will continue until the atmosphere is at the same humidity as the clay. If the atmosphere is freely circulating the clay will eventually lose so much moisture that it will become very hard and unworkable. The warmth of your hands and the absorbency of the surface you are working on will also cause the clay to lose moisture. To keep clay damp and workable, the surrounding atmosphere must be kept equally damp. This is best managed by covering the clay with a damp cloth, and a further tight covering of plastic sheeting will keep the clay in a workable condition for a long time. For the same reasons clay is best stored in an airtight container such as a plastic bin with a lid. Hard clay can be made soft again by adding water but this is a process which cannot be hurried. The dry clay should be broken into small pieces in a suitable container and then covered with water. It will take time for the water to penetrate the clay so the smaller the pieces the better. Short clays will soften more quickly because they are more open than fat clays. Some very fine clays are quite reluctant to re-absorb water, probably because the clay swells and tightens the surface layers of the lump and slows the entry of more water. This is sometimes the problem with semi-dry clays and it is often better to fully dry and crush the clay before soaking. The water will then swell and crumble the clay and cause a more rapid penetration of water. After soaking, the water content of the clay will still be unevenly distributed. Free water must be poured off and the clay must be mixed by kneading it like dough. This is called 'wedging'. If the clay is too wet for use at this time it will need to be dried off for a while and then re-wedged. If wedging is carried out on an absorbent surface, such as an asbestos sheet, this will help to remove excess moisture more rapidly. It is essential that clay be kept in a suitable working condition. Of course, it is much easier to manage this by careful storage, but clay will always benefit from wedging before use.

By varying the water content a complete range of clay consistencies can be obtained, from a thin creamy fluid, through a stiff paste and pliable lump, to the leather-hard and finally rock-hard state. The majority of shaping processes require the clay to be in a reasonably soft and pliable condition, but it is essential to learn as quickly as possible how to judge when the clay is in the right condition to most easily and effectively carry out the particular operation you intend. The product will reflect your judgement and you must learn to work in harmony with the characteristic qualities and changing conditions of the clay. Sometimes you will need to delay drying and at other times you will have to wait until the clay has stiffened sufficiently for the next operation to be carried out.

Fig. 4   Objects made from clays of various consistencies

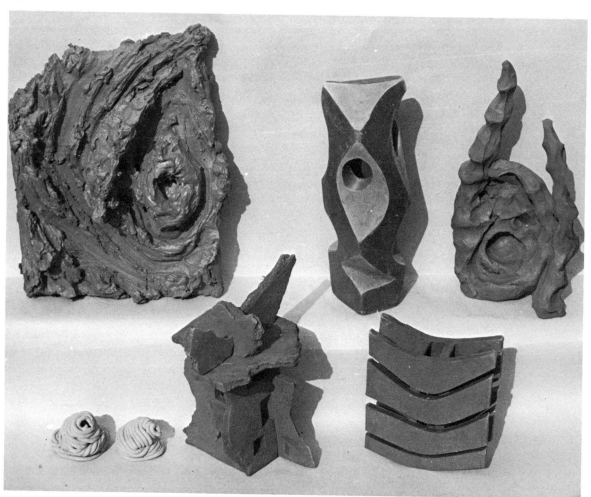

8

The characteristics of clay

At this point it might be very helpful to put aside the blinkers of convention and explore fundamentally what clay will and will not do in its various states of fluidity, plasticity and hardness. In this way you will discover for yourself why some of the traditional clay treatments exist and you may even discover some quite unexpected ways of using clay effectively. Enjoy the feel of clay and only use implements when you have thoroughly explored what you can do with your hands. The implements you use to shape clay, whether they be your hands, a kitchen fork, a plastic bottle, a saw blade, the heel of your shoe, a potato peeler, a piece of splintered wood or an electric masonry drill, will leave their own characteristic imprint.

Think carefully about the surfaces on which you are working. Damp clay will stick tightly to non-absorbent surfaces such as formica and this will strongly influence your manner of working with the clay. Try working on surfaces of varying absorbency such as wood, asbestos, stone, plaster, cloth, etc. so that the clay can spread or shrink or be turned and built outwards or upwards. Clay shaped in the hands will naturally assume a different form from clay worked on a flat surface. Explore what happens when you combine clays of different consistency. You will never exhaust all the possibilities, but freed from the constraints of having to *make* something, you will certainly make some discoveries about clay which will be invaluable to your further progress.

Even the seeming 'failures' of such experimentation can be most useful if you approach the results with a questioning mind. You will make some very personal and individual discoveries but there are certain underlying fundamental factors which are inescapable.

1. Clay shrinks as it dries.
2. The wetter the clay the greater the drying shrinkage.
3. Short clays shrink less than fat clays of equal moisture content.
4. Clay will crack as it dries unless it is free to take up shrinkage movement.
5. Even drying reduces shrinkage tensions.
6. The greater the difference in the moisture content of clays the greater will be the resistance to secure joining.
7. Increased water content reduces the self-supportive capability of clay.
8. Clay becomes brittle as it dries.
9. Damp clays can only be securely joined if the meeting surfaces are adequately roughened, moistened and integrated.

The latter point requires a little expansion. Clay is composed of minute sheet-like particles which interlock. When moisture is present these particles attract a thin film of water to themselves and are able to ride over each other producing the characteristic plasticity of damp clay. At the smoothed surface of a piece of damp clay the majority of particles are lying flat. If a similar piece of smooth,

Fig. 5 Damp clays can be joined securely only if the meeting surfaces are adequately roughened, moistened and integrated

damp clay is pressed in contact it will stick initially because of the thin film of moisture present, but when this surface moisture evaporates the clay will fall apart. Only by disturbing the clay particles through scratching the surfaces to be joined and by introducing a little extra moisture will the clay particles of both pieces have opportunity to interlock and form a secure joint.

Firing clay

Many of the clay products of your experimentation will crack up as they dry and others will be impossibly fragile, but there may be a few which are sufficiently sturdy and interesting to bake (fire). In any case it will be interesting to see what happens to the clay when fired. Do not expect that everything you fire will necessarily survive. The stresses of heating (and cooling) will reveal any structural weakness, but careful management will minimize disappointments. Whether you are using the simplest or most sophisticated means of firing your work there are two rules which must always be followed:

1. Ensure that the objects to be fired are thoroughly atmosphere-dried.
2. Fire very slowly until all free water has been driven from the clay (at least 1 hour for the first 100°C).

10

These rules must be observed because the water always present in clay, no matter how thoroughly it has been dried in the atmosphere, will form steam at 100°C. If the steam is produced slowly enough it will filter its way through and out of the clay. If the steam cannot escape quickly enough it will set up pressure which will burst the clay—quite violently sometimes. Short clays which have been opened with sand will lose their moisture more readily than fat clays which have much smaller passageways between their particles. Thick-sectioned clay objects are at risk because the water contained in the clay must migrate further to escape at the surface.

Sawdust firing

Clay must be heated to a minimum of 500–600°C before it changes to pottery. An ordinary domestic cooker is not hot enough but you can very easily and quickly make a simple and efficient kiln. You will need:

1. Some dry, slow-burning fuel, e.g. sawdust, peat, leaves, bark, rotten wood, etc.
2. Some means of containing the burning fuel and clay objects, e.g. bricks, paving slabs, an empty oil drum, a bucket.
3. Some means of regulating ventilation.

It may seem strange that a gently smouldering sawdust heap will produce more heat than a domestic oven but if you are in any doubt just submerge a fired object in water; if you have achieved the required temperature (500–600°C) the object will remain intact, if you have failed to reach the necessary temperature the object will re-absorb water and collapse into a soft clay heap. In pottery terms you will not reach high temperature by this means and the objects will still be fairly brittle and soft. Some kinds of pottery, namely stoneware and porcelain, are fired to twice this temperature (1200–1350°C) but more sophisticated firing methods are used. It is by no means certain that your locally discovered clay would withstand such high temperatures and careful testing would be necessary before you attempted to work at higher temperatures.

The simple kiln can be as large or small as necessary provided each object is surrounded by two or three inches of the slow-burning fuel. It is necessary to make a retaining enclosure to conserve heat and to prevent strong winds from fanning the fire into too much life. Also, it is helpful if the ventilation holes are adjustable so that the fire can be kept burning gently even if the wind varies. Light the fire at the point or points where there is free air access. Make a small loose twist of newspaper and lightly embed one end in the fuel (sawdust etc.). When you light the paper the fuel should smoulder quite gently. Do not expect large flames.

Working within these guidelines there are a variety of possibilities. The diagrams and pictures show some examples. Your choice will be influenced by

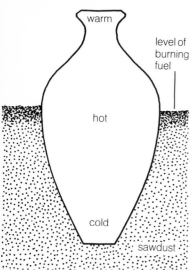

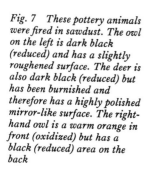

materials available but be careful to observe the principles of dry fuel, dry clay and slow heating and cooling. As will be seen later, with most other forms of firing the *whole* clay object is slowly heated and brought to the required firing temperature. With this simple firing process it is probable that as the fuel slowly burns down only *part* of the object will be fully fired whilst other parts of the object are still heating up. This will give rise to certain stresses due to the chemical and physical changes that take place in the object, but careful management of the firing will reduce the stresses to a minimum.

Oxidation and reduction

The majority of objects fired by this means will usually be black or dark grey in colour but in some places you will probably notice much lighter patches of pale grey, red or pink. Careful observation will show that these lighter patches of colour occur in the more ventilated areas (near ventilating tubes, etc.). The dark colours are, in part, due to carbon, present in the smoke, being trapped in the clay. Also, the carbon in smoke tends to use up oxygen and any iron in the clay

Fig. 6 *Heat distribution diagram showing the progressive firing of an object in slow-burning sawdust. Objects will expand as they are heated and contract as they are cooled. Parts of the same pot will be expanding as others are contracting during a sawdust firing because the fuel burns down slowly. However, since the heat gradient is fairly even, most pots can be expected to survive*

Fig. 7 *These pottery animals were fired in sawdust. The owl on the left is dark black (reduced) and has a slightly roughened surface. The deer is also dark black (reduced) but has been burnished and therefore has a highly polished mirror-like surface. The right-hand owl is a warm orange in front (oxidized) but has a black (reduced) area on the back*

12

will become black (reduced) iron. Where the atmosphere is less smoky and better ventilated any iron present in the clay will turn red (oxidize) producing the lighter colour variations. These colour variations can be very attractive and with a little thoughtful arrangement of ventilation they can be encouraged to develop if you so wish. Layers of slow- and fast-burning fuels can be experimented with, e.g. the clay objects can be embedded in peat to ensure slow heating but beneath this layer there could be dried grass which will burn faster and less smokily and which might produce more interesting colour variations. Perhaps kindling wood could be fed in beneath the fire once the slow-burning fuel had done its job.

Burnishing

You will not be able to glaze objects fired by this means, the temperatures are too low and the atmosphere is too smoky. However, some very attractive surface qualities can be obtained by burnishing the clay when it is still damp but quite hard. Use a spoon or knife handle and rub firmly in small circles. If you catch the clay at the right hardness it is possible to produce a really attractive, smooth, shiny surface.

CASE HISTORY 1:
a sawdust kiln firing

Having made a collection of small pots and models from the local clay we dried them thoroughly in the atmosphere. We then managed to find twenty ordinary building bricks with which we made a small enclosure two bricks square and two bricks deep. A layer of fine sawdust was poured in to a depth of about four inches and the dried pots were embedded in the sawdust layer. More sawdust was poured over the pots and the last pots were embedded in the sawdust. Four bricks were placed across the corners of the square to narrow the brick enclosure. More sawdust was poured in and a twist of newspaper was partly buried in the top of the sawdust pile. This was set alight and when the flames from the paper died down the sawdust had started to smoulder. A dustbin lid was placed over the opening and smoke slowly curled up through the gaps in the bricks.

Within fourteen hours the sawdust had slowly burned away and the fire-hardened pots were removed, still warm, from amongst the ashes. All these pots were dark black but had changed from clay to pottery with the heat.

At the same time we started another sawdust firing in a metal bin. It was carried out in exactly the same manner as above, but instead of bricks we used the bin to enclose the fire and two roofing tiles to partly close in the top. The pots fired perfectly well but the sawdust went out before it had completely burned away to the bottom of the bin. Obviously a little more ventilation was needed.

13

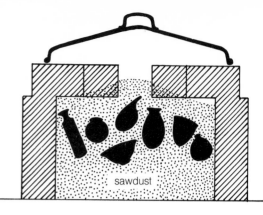

Fig. 9 Diagram of a simple sawdust-fired kiln. The fire is retained by any suitable enclosure—bucket, bricks, etc.—and pots are embedded in the sawdust, about $2\frac{1}{2}$ inches apart. A lighted twist of newspaper is used to start the sawdust burning from the top. When the sawdust has smouldered away the firing is complete

Fig. 8 A sawdust firing is started. Dry, raw clay pots are embedded in sawdust. The fire is retained by bricks, covered with a dustbin lid and allowed to smoulder slowly

Fig. 10 A sawdust firing completed in a metal bin

CASE HISTORY 2:
a clamp kiln firing

For this firing we made use of a small pit which we had dug in the ground (about as wide and a little deeper than a dustbin lid). Three pieces of scrap metal tubing were laid into the pit and pointed in different directions. A small wood fire was then kindled in the bottom of the pit. When it was burning well we piled on some sawdust which deadened the flames; the smoke issuing from the ventilating tubes indicated that the sawdust was smouldering well. Then we gently embedded the pots in the sawdust pile and covered them with another layer of sawdust. The original turf was used to cover the pile and, as it threatened to rain, we covered the clamp with a dustbin lid. The wind was obviously carrying air down the tubes to the fire at the base of the pit. No smoke issued from the tube which faced into the wind but a steady curl of smoke rose from the other ventilation tubes. Within fourteen hours the fire had burned out.

We raked amongst the embers and found our pots and models. This time they were not all black but had some interesting patches of grey, buff and red on them. We noticed that the lighter colours appeared on the faces of the pots nearest to the ventilation tubes. All were well fired and probably harder than the pots from the first firing.

Fig. 11 A clamp kiln. Ventilation tubes lead to the bottom of the pit where a kindling-wood fire is burning (see smoke at tube on left). Pots and models are embedded in sawdust above the fire. Finally turf is laid over the sawdust heap which is left to burn slowly

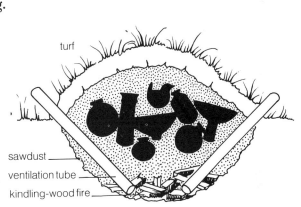

turf

sawdust

ventilation tube

kindling-wood fire

Fig. 12 Diagram of a clamp kiln

CASE HISTORY 3:

the sophisticated sawdust kiln

Fig. 13 A 'sophisticated' sawdust kiln under construction. Note the ventilation tubes, wire-netting 'safety net', and the bricks at the base which will be withdrawn for the final wood firing to produce oxidized areas

Fig. 14 Diagram of a 'sophisticated' sawdust kiln. The clay objects are supported on layers of wire netting. Ventilation tubes are arranged to produce interesting dark and light patches of reduction and oxidation. Slow-burning fuels surround the pots but they are sandwiched between faster-burning layers, and the firing is completed with a brisk wood firing fed through the stoking ports at the kiln base when the sawdust and shavings have burned away

We liked the colour variations produced by the clamp kiln and decided to try to improve on these qualities. We made another brick enclosure two bricks square, but this time poured in a layer of chips and shavings at the bottom of the enclosure in the hope that they would burn more cleanly and brighter than the sawdust. We then poured in a thin layer of sawdust and placed some wire netting across the bricks to stop the pots falling against each other during the firing. Ventilation tubes were placed in position and the pots were stood around the tubes in a bed of sawdust. More sawdust was poured over the pots and then more shavings, thus forming a sawdust 'sandwich'. Another layer of sawdust, wire netting, pots and shavings were added and, after the sawdust had been lighted, the top was partly closed with a dustbin lid.

When the kiln had nearly burned out, ten hours later, we pulled out four loose bricks from the base of the kiln and fed in some small pieces of kindling wood which burned brightly, producing flames which licked out around the dustbin lid.

The pots from this kiln were fired even harder and had some very exciting colour variations.

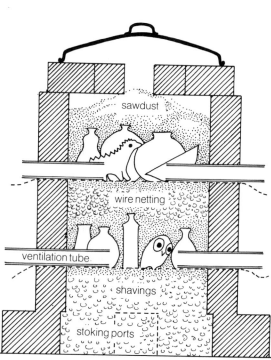

16

2 Prehistoric pottery

The very earliest known examples of fired clay objects date back almost 100 000 years, to the last Ice Age, but a very considerable time elapsed before pottery became securely established as a common craft. Freedom of movement was more important to the nomadic hunter than a collection of fragile domestic pottery, but in the Neolithic period, when a more settled form of existence evolved as a result of the development of farming methods, circumstances favoured the development of pottery as a domestic craft. There is no single origin of the craft, but as early civilized communities developed in different parts of the world over a wide time span, so the development of pottery flourished.

Because pottery objects are durable there are plentiful examples in existence today which give fairly clear evidence of the wide range of items made many thousands of years ago. What is by no means as clearly evident are the processes and procedures by which these objects were made. The earliest firing methods can only be guessed at. The fire-hardened, clay-lined hearths which have been discovered may have been sites of domestic fires for cooking or warmth, just as they may have been the sites of primitive kilns; or they may have been one and the same thing. Some of the most reliable information comes from the pottery remains which reflect the materials and processes by and with which they were fashioned. Some detective work at the museum will give interesting information that might prove very useful.

Amongst the very earliest examples of prehistoric pottery there are some clumsy, lumpy looking examples which are surprisingly crude when compared with other examples of prehistoric man's craftsmanship. Some of the implements made of bone are beautifully shaped and finely decorated, but close inspection of the pots shows that even the clay used is very coarse and full of quite large bits and pieces which must have made the clay quite difficult to

Fig. 15 *A prehistoric funerary urn made from very coarse, gritty clay.* By kind permission of the University Museum of Archaeology and Ethnology, Cambridge

Fig. 16 *A paleolithic bone carving.* By kind permission of the University Museum of Archaeology and Ethnology, Cambridge

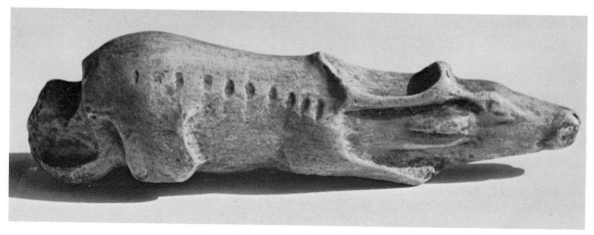

shape with any degree of refinement. It may seem strange that prehistoric man bothered to use such rough clay, especially when there must have been many sources of much finer, smooth clays which he could have chosen to use. Sometimes the bits and pieces embedded in the clay look like fine gravel and sometimes there are white flakes that look remarkably like fragments of shells. Small pores, pockets and pits can often be seen in the pots, as if particles have dropped out or burned out of the clay. In fact these 'bits and pieces' were intentionally mixed with the clay to 'temper' it, as mentioned in the previous chapter; prehistoric man also discovered that tempered clay did not warp, shrink or crack so much. The coarse particles opened the pores of the clay so that the moisture it contained could escape quickly and evenly, both as the clay dried in the atmosphere and during the firing. This was very important since the pots were probably fired very quickly, in about two or three hours; the moisture had to be able to escape rapidly otherwise it would have burst the clay apart.

Much of the tempering used was quite small in size and cannot be seen with the naked eye. It included sand, crushed rock and pieces of broken pot, ash, plant fibres, and even feathers! Unfortunately, the type and amount of tempering material used has its effect on the plasticity of the clay, which becomes gradually more crumbly as more tempering material is added. High plasticity was unnecessary in prehistoric times because the pots were most probably made by squeezing, rolling, pinching, beating and scraping the clay into shape, but the tempering particles had to be sufficiently small to cure rather than to cause cracking. Too much tempering can seriously weaken the dry and fired strength of the clay, so a point of balance was struck which enabled the clay to be both shaped and fired satisfactorily. Sand may seem to be the most obvious choice of tempering material and it often occurs naturally mixed with clays. It has a fine particle size but the particles are rather rounded in shape. Jagged particles such as crushed shell, which prehistoric man used, would have worked well at the temperatures to which he fired his pots (i.e. 750–800°C), but fired more slowly and to only slightly higher temperatures the shells would have changed chemically and caused harm to the pots.

Another feature of interest in prehistoric pottery is that nearly all the forms made were basically rounded. This may seem strange at first when we remember that these pots were not made on the potter's wheel. A wheel of any sort was unknown to man at this time. The pots were hand-built and it would have been just as easy to make them square or rectangular. Probably it was noted that rounded forms survived best—a blow to such a pot is transmitted around the form without interruption, whereas stress concentrates at the corners of an angular form causing it to break more easily. Also, clay is soft and plastic and forms a curve more naturally and comfortably than it forms an angle, especially if the clay has a high proportion of tempering material in it.

The patchy black, brown-red, yellow and grey shades of the prehistoric pots give further information about the way in which they were fired. The sawdust

Fig. 17 Two bronze-age mugs. Note the refinement of the right-hand example and the crudity of the left-hand one. The differences could be a reflection of different firing methods, different clays or social and cultural evolution. By kind permission of the University Museum of Archaeology and Ethnology, Cambridge

firings mentioned in chapter 1 produced pots with a similar colour range but perhaps somewhat darker overall, except where the fire was more fully oxidized in the areas surrounding the ventilating tubes. The prehistoric pots were probably fired in big, open, blazing bonfires, but it would still have been necessary to prevent sudden heating and cooling, so slow and fast-burning fuels would have been used at the appropriate times. The slow-burning fuels probably produced much smoke which would have caused the darkened patches of colour. Very similar methods are still used today by the more primitive cultures in parts of Nigeria and Africa and by the American Indians.[1]

It is difficult, when viewing prehistoric pots through the glass of a showcase in a twentieth-century museum, to imagine them in daily use some thousands of years ago. They were never used at table to sip coffee with a genteelly crooked little finger! To imagine them used for a drink of mammoth's blood, clutched in the iron grasp of a wild-eyed, half ape-like creature crouched at the back of a dank cave in the dim light of a sputtering animal-fat candle, might be equally far removed from the truth. The pots themselves are evidence of an intelligent reasoning—tempered clays to improve drying and firing performance; strong

[1] Bernard Leach *A Potter's Book* (Faber & Faber, London), pp. 179–180.
Fontana, Robinson, Cormack & Leavitt *Papago Indian Pottery* (Washington).
Cardew *Pioneer Pottery* (Longman, London), pp. 76–78.

rounded forms to survive the knocks of daily use. The first crude handles, in time, became more delicate, graceful and refined; symptoms of improved firing methods which increasingly hardened and strengthened the pottery thus allowing it to withstand the stresses of leverage better. Fingernails, stones, bone and plaited cords were used to make patterns in the soft clay surfaces—sure signs of a more ordered existence which gave man freedom to express his creative ideas. Painted decoration, using carefully selected rich iron-bearing earths, was used at an early period. The precision, control and vitality of such decoration is the more impressive when we remember that prehistoric man had no fine sable-haired brushes to use. His tools and materials were of the simplest kind, fashioned from the resources of his environment, yet the pots and models he made were often very beautiful in form and decoration.

How clay was formed
Basically all clays are decomposed rock. The rock concerned is called feldspar. These rocks were formed and decomposition began millions of years ago at a time when the climate and physical forces at work were very different from those which exist today. Hot gases and steam belched from the earth and frequent volcanic activity threw up molten masses which cooled slowly and were often subjected to extreme variations in pressure and temperature. The decomposed feldspathic rock which remains where it was formed is a very pure but rather large-particled clay known as primary clay (such as the white-firing china clays of the West Country). However, most clays, over a long period of time, have been weathered by wind, rain, frost and sun and then carried away by small streams into rivers, lakes, estuaries and oceans. This action performed a sorting and grading process. The larger and heavier clay particles were deposited on the stream and river beds; only the very smallest particles were carried on to the lakes and oceans where the water current slackened and the clay particles eventually settled into beds of fine secondary clays. These clays will have lost much of their soluble ingredients to the water by which they were transported but can be expected to have gained all manner of other impurities during their journey. Iron is a very common impurity and can be identified by the yellow, orange and red hues which it gives the clay. Sometimes the iron colouration may be disguised by decayed plants and other organic matter in the clay which will often cause it to turn to shades of grey, blue and black. Since the face of the earth has been frequently resculptured, the clays on today's hilltops may well have been raised from the lake beds of a million years ago as the earth's crust folded and buckled in times past. Also, the world's first and most powerful bulldozers, the ice-caps, did some mighty earth moving during the ice ages.

Thus it is apparent that although all clays have a common origin they can be expected to vary considerably. There will be differences of colour which can be seen and differences of texture which we can feel, but there are other differences which will only become evident when the clay is fired. These variations are due to the loss of clay solubles during weathering and to the 'impurities' which are deposited with the secondary clays. They affect the 'meltability' (fusibility) of clay when it is heated. All clays will eventually melt to a glassy state if they are heated to sufficiently high temperatures; the hardening and vitrifying of fired clays are the first signs of melting and are in some measure essential to the fired strength of clay.

Suppliers of clay for pottery select and blend their clays so that they will have the desired characteristics. For low-temperature firing you will need an earthenware clay which will develop sufficient fired strength, but you will have to pay for the cost of clay preparation and transport too. Small quantities of clay may be sufficiently expensive today to provide a strong incentive for you to gather your own. In any case, I think this is very much part of the fun, and good earthenware clays are very readily available. It is much less likely that you will find very refractory (not very meltable) clays. If your pots are still very soft after firing and have no ring to them you may assume either that they have not been fired to a high enough temperature or that the clay you are using is a refractory clay—more suitable for the stoneware and raku work described later.

If you have the facilities for making a good bonfire then you can recapture the experiences of prehistoric potters.

CASE HISTORY 4:
an open firing

The clay

A red earthenware clay was used to build the one large pot which we fired in the open kiln. Basically, the clay was fine textured and very plastic but we added a considerable amount of sand and finely-crushed fired clay (this is called 'grog' and can be bought ready crushed in various grades from dust to quite coarse particles, or you can make your own by crushing broken flower pots, bricks, etc.) until the clay was very open in texture but still just sufficiently plastic to shape. The sand and grog were slightly damped before mixing so that they did not dry out the clay too much. It is impossible to give an exact guide to the amount added because clays vary considerably in their basic plasticity and may already contain quantities of sand and grog, so you will have to do as we did and add as much as you can without making it too crumbly (short) to use.

Forming the pot

To make the pot we used a very traditional forming method known as 'coiling'. The clay was squeezed into sausages and then rolled on a flat, semi-absorbent surface into long rounded lengths. A generous clear working surface is needed for rolling so that the to-and-fro rolling action is free. Short rolling movements

Fig. 18 Wedging sand and grog into the clay

tend to produce oval sections. Of course, prehistoric man, like the primitive potters of today, had no such working surface and probably rolled the clay coils between his hands in a vertical manner.

The coils of clay were then built up one upon the other and each coil was very firmly thumbed into the one below, the pressure being contained by support from the other hand on the outside of the form. The clay had to be sufficiently damp to allow the clay coils to be merged together thoroughly; any weak joints would split apart during the firing. Coil was built upon coil; sometimes a coil was made a little wider than the one below and the form was thus widened, and narrowing was achieved by reversing the process. This particular pot was built upside down; the first coil laid down was later to become the rim. Had we started with the shallow curve of the base the increasing weight of the clay being built above would have caused the form to collapse. Very sudden changes of direction in the form were also avoided for the same reason. If you want to build more exaggerated curved forms you must be patient and wait for the lower part of the form to stiffen sufficiently to support the stresses imposed on it.

23

The piled-up layers of clay grow somewhat like knitting. Each coil will reflect the confidence, control and assurance with which it is applied. Times will come when the form will waver and sway beneath your hands and you must learn how to keep the form in balance, when to pause, when and how to change direction. Sometimes the form may need to be gently beaten into its final shape from the inside or outside. The back of a hair brush or wooden spoon are useful tools for this purpose and will strengthen the shape by compacting the clay surface. The coils may be left showing, for their texture qualities, on the outside of the form but until you are confident that the coils are really securely joined it may be safer to thumb them together on both sides of the clay wall. This particular pot was smoothed together inside and out, beaten true with a wooden spoon and then a band of decorative texture was scratched with a fork into the smooth, soft clay. The textured band was also lightly beaten to avoid a scratchy surface which would be unpleasant to the touch. When the pot was firm enough to stand upright the rim was wiped round and round with a damp chamois leather to smooth and true it.

The open firing

Fig. 19 An open firing—
stage 1. The dry pot is inverted
and glowing embers are placed
under it to provide a gentle heat

Fig. 20 An open firing—
stage 2. Slow-burning fuel, i.e.
dead wood and green lawn trimmings are built up around the pot

When the pot had dried thoroughly we stood it rim down on four half-bricks over a few gently glowing embers. Patiently and very slowly we fed some pieces of rotten wood beneath the pot, gradually warming it. It was a rather cold spring morning and we were anxious about the sudden gusts of chill wind that swept the garden, so we built up a protective wall of rotten logs and sprinkled fresh lawn trimmings over the upturned pot base. Soon the lawn trimmings steamed, turned brown and smouldered, showing that the pot was warming

up. The surrounding logs started to smoke and smoulder. About an hour later we were able to add some dry pieces of pinewood and saw the first small flames lick round the pot. Too much flame was prevented with more handfuls of lawn trimmings and the pot was again lost in smoke. We had to restrain our natural impatience. Gradually more dry wood was added and more flame appeared. The lawn trimmings burned away quickly now as the flames danced round the pot. Then, to our dismay, a sudden gust of cold wind caught the partly exposed side of the pot and we heard a muffled but ominous crack! We quickly protected the exposed pot with more wood and soon the flames leaped and swirled in the air. Sometimes we could see parts of the pot glowing red-hot in the centre of the fire and decided that the fire had by now done its job, so we let it burn down and heaped more lawn trimmings and any other slow-burning fuel we could find over the fired pot to avoid sudden cooling. The whole process took about three hours from start to finish.

The pot was well and truly fired. At a guess I would think it must have reached about 800°C. The colour of the pot was really magnificent; there were bright patches of orange-red contrasting with areas of deep black and grey. Unfortunately there was a crack of about 6 inches which travelled vertically down from the rim, the result of the chill wind catching the exposed pot. Had the crack been caused by faulty construction it would have run horizontally around the pot in the direction of the applied coils.

We had demonstrated to our own satisfaction that it was quite possible to obtain a good firing by the open-fire method, just as prehistoric man had done. Obviously a good, warm and windless summer day would improve the chance of complete success but the result was very encouraging.

Fig. 21 An open firing—stage 3. Furiously burning, dry, resinous wood at the height of the firing

Fig. 22 Open firing complete. Note the contrasting areas of oxidation and reduction

More about coiling

The method of coiling is suitable for making very large or fairly small forms and for both symmetrical and assymmetrical shapes. It is a comparatively slow way of making a pot but this may be a hidden advantage since there is more time to contemplate and consider the form as it slowly evolves. Although it is a time-honoured method of forming it is a very fertile one where individuality of expression is concerned.

The coils need not necessarily be uniformly rounded in section, indeed some irregularities may add excitement to the texture of the surface. Some potters lap the coils for strength of join, and deeper, flatter coils may be worked into the form and perhaps be looped and snaked, leaving decorative perforations. Pellets may also be inserted between the coils. The variations of form and texture are limitless.

Good coil pots require a sympathetic feeling for clay which will come only through continued experience. The learner is well advised to attempt simple forms initially. It is not exactly easy to make an even roll of clay and somehow the form has a nasty habit of taking its own direction in the hands of a beginner. If this is your experience then you may achieve more immediate satisfaction by using some sort of former for coiling. A wide cardboard tube that you can easily reach into (e.g. lengths cut from the centre of a lino-roll core), a cardboard box or a colander could be used to coil in. The coils, which need not be especially regular in section, can be laid in position and the exposed surface welded firmly together. When the clay dries and shrinks it can be withdrawn from the support. If you have not pressed too hard and if the clay is not too soft the coiled textured surface will remain as an exciting exterior surface. As previously mentioned, the form may be built from the base upwards or from the rim downwards and additional variety of form will result if the coils are built up on a curved instead of a flat baseboard.

Pinched pots

The coiled-pot layers were pinched, stroked, squeezed and beaten together, but the smaller prehistoric pots such as the beakers were probably made from just one lump of clay, turned in the palm of one hand and pinched into shape by squeezing the clay wall between the thumb and fingers of the other hand. The size of such a pot is limited to some extent by the size of your hand and the depth to which your fingers can reach into the shape you are forming, so begin with a fairly small ball of clay which will nestle comfortably into the palm of your hand. This may sound easy and is often suggested as a good introductory exercise for aspiring potters, but it is more difficult than it sounds. Somehow, despite your original intention, the shape opens wider and wider, the edges fray and the product is an uninspiring ashtray instead of an elegant chalice!

Success depends to a large extent upon an understanding derived from

Fig. 23   This coil pot has a relaxed control and the character of the clay and process are being allowed to make their own contribution

Fig. 24   Coiled pots formed inside a cardboard cylinder

Fig. 25   The pinch pot is turned in one hand and pinched into shape by squeezing the clay wall between the thumb and fingers of the other hand

27

experience in handling clay. Generally, rhythmic pinching should start from the floor of the pot. To keep the mouth of the pot narrow, stroke inwards with the fingers against the thumb. Sometimes it will be necessary to hold the rim and neck of the pot between the fingers and thumbs of both hands and compress together to narrow the neck. Should you want an open bowl shape then start pinching and thinning from the rim to the base. As the walls get thinner you will find that a deeper bowl results if it is worked upside down and a shallower one if it is thinned the right way up. This is due in part to the gravitational pull on the thin walls. If cracks appear as you work the clay try using softer clay from the start; liberal applications of water will only make the pot slippery and the water will not readily penetrate the clay. Always start with a newly wedged piece of clay. Never roll up the previous failure and use it again because it will have lost too much moisture and will soon crack (a pair of rubber gloves may be useful if your hands always dry the clay too much). See just how much you can thin the clay walls by pinching, and when the clay gets very thin stand it to one side until it stiffens enough to work on again. It may be necessary to stand the pot on a cup in order to take the weight off the base and avoid it sagging or collapsing. The shape can be trued and the form altered or textured by beating with a ruler or spoon etc., and then perhaps burnished when it is firm enough.

Making a whistle

Pinching and coiling methods may be combined if desired. The whistles (see fig. 27) were made by joining two pinched pots. A solid mouth-piece was grafted on and a lollypop stick was used to open the mouth-piece and pierce obliquely into the thumb-pot chamber. With the lollypop stick still in position a slanting cut was made toward the mouth-piece down to the stick, thus forming a cutting edge to split the wind from the mouth-piece. The lollypop stick was then withdrawn and the clay cutting edge depressed *very* slightly. The exact position of the cutting edge is vital. The whistle produced will vary

Fig. 26 This pinch-pot whistle in the form of an owl produces three notes, the eye holes acting as keys. The tail forms the mouthpiece and the whistle aperture is situated in the back

in pitch according to the length of the resonating wind. If holes are pierced elsewhere around the whistle body the air will escape at these points and the vibrating air column will be effectively shortened, thus raising the pitch of the note. Since the holes are made in the damp clay they can be enlarged, reduced, filled in and shifted to produce the required notes which remain reasonably faithful even after firing. Flutes and recorders can be made in clay. Rattles, bells, rasps and drums are also possibilities if you are musically inclined.

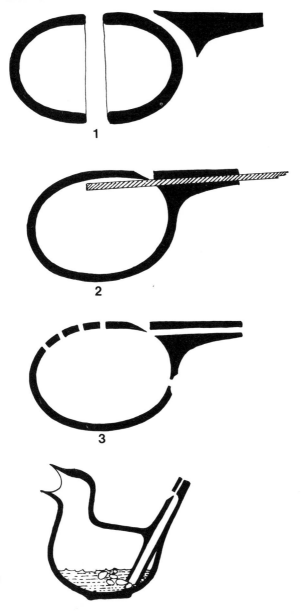

Fig. 27 Diagram of a whistle. (1) Join two thumb pots rim to rim and graft on a solid mouthpiece; (2) Use a lollipop stick to pierce the mouthpiece. With the stick in position, cut a wedge through the wall down to the stick; (3) Remove the stick and gently adjust the cutting edge until a whistle is produced. More holes may be pierced with a nail to vary the pitch.

Bird whistle variation. Make a straight tube whistle. Insert the tube almost to the base of an open-necked vessel. Partly fill the vessel with water; when the whistle is blown the escaping air will cause the water to rise and fall in the tube, thus varying the pitch

Figurines

In addition to the early pottery vessels made by prehistoric man there are also many examples of small clay figurines. It would be difficult to say with certainty exactly what these figurines were used for. They may have been used as charms or for ceremonial purposes but certainly they are very attractive. It would seem that they were often pinched out from a single lump of clay and only the decorative details were added in the form of little pellets and rolls of clay. Perhaps prehistoric man discovered that it is difficult to join clay very securely so the pinching-out method of modelling was preferred. The size of the figurines may have been limited by the fact that thick sections of clay are more difficult to dry evenly and quickly and consequently they often blow up during rapid firing.

If you feel you would like to attempt making models then try pinching out from a single lump to start with. Allow the clay to make its own unique contribution to the quality of the modelling. If it is necessary to add on additional lumps of clay, scratch up the two surfaces to be joined and apply a little liquid clay (slip) before firmly wriggling the two pieces together (see fig. 5). If you want to make larger models that you intend to fire they will have to be hollowed out. They can either be made solid and then hollowed out from underneath or they can be made from basic thumb-pot shapes or sheets of clay. A totally closed hollow form must be punctured at some point to allow the air to escape as it expands during firing.

Model making can be very satisfying. It is a good starting point for beginners and young children because it is a relatively uncomplicated process which will encourage a good understanding of some of the basic qualities of clay.

Fig. 28 Prehistoric model of an antelope. By kind permission of the University Museum of Archaeology and Ethnology, Cambridge

Fig. 29 'Duet'. Solid clay models which preserve a lively quality in the relaxed method of their modelling

30

Fig. 30 'Court scene' group worked in solid clay

Fig. 31   These are 'magic flowers that glow in the midnight garden'. The centrepiece is a nightlight around which the 'flowers' were built, as part of a group activity, with simple rolls and small pinched-out sheets of clay

3 Shapes from clay sheets

There is an unlimited variety of forms, shapes and objects which can be made from sheets of clay. The only constraints that will be encountered are those imposed by:

1. The nature and condition of the clay. Is the clay hard enough or soft enough, too short or too fat to comfortably assume the intended form?
2. The suitability of the form to this method of construction.

These are considerations fundamental to all pottery processes and success will depend largely upon a clear understanding of them. Within limits, it is possible to adjust the nature and condition of the clay, to modify the form or to use a more appropriate forming method, but the craftsman must also be able to adapt his ideas.

Forming sheets

The clay will need to be in a moderately soft condition if it is to be formed into sheets, and the most rapid way to make the sheets is by the wire cutting method. For this, a length of steel or brass wire (which will not rust) or tough nylon fishing line will be needed; about twelve inches will probably be enough. To stop the wire cutting into the fingers as it is pulled it is helpful to secure a button, small piece of wood, or a curtain ring to each end. After the clay has been thoroughly wedged it should be knocked into a rough block and finally brought down firmly in good contact with the working surface. Now place wooden guide slats on opposite sides of the lump. The slats should be between $\frac{1}{4}$ and $\frac{3}{8}$ of an inch thick and about 18 inches long. Draw the cutting wire tight, press it down on the guide slats and draw it towards you. The weight of clay block above the wire should be sufficient to hold it in position as you cut, provided the clay is not too stiff. The block can now be lifted and placed to one side of the cut sheet, the guide slats can be repositioned and the process can be repeated as many times as necessary.

An alternative method of forming a sheet is to thin the clay by compression. A dry, wooden rolling-pin will be needed. The clay must be soft enough to spread but not so wet that it sticks to the rolling-pin and the working surface must be semi-absorbent. This is a more strenuous process so try to judge the clay quantity with reasonable accuracy. It is a waste of time and energy to roll out more clay than is necessary. Start by squashing and spreading the lump with the weight of your body over the heel of your hand and encourage the clay to spread into the required shape, i.e. long and narrow, circular etc. This again will save time and energy. Be sure to lift up the clay from time to time so that it does not become tightly stuck to the working surface. If the clay begins to stick down as the working surface becomes damp, move it to a drier place. It is often helpful to roll clay out on cloth or hessian to prevent sticking, but it will still need lifting from time to time. The wooden rolling-pin will help to even up the thickness and smooth the surface of the sheet. It may be used across wooden guide slats to ensure an even thickness but with experience guide slats become unnecessary. Repeatedly change direction with the rolling-pin so that it does not merely rise and fall with the contours of the clay, but flattens and spreads the raised areas.

Both methods described here produce sheets of clay which are similar in appearance but this is only a superficial similarity. The rolled clay sheet is much more compressed and compacted in consequence of the way in which it was made. The clay particles will be more aligned and the sheet will be stronger and more able to withstand some of the subsequent stresses of the forming processes. The best of both sheet-forming procedures can be gained by wire cutting somewhat thicker slabs and then rolling them to the required finished thickness with a rolling-pin.

Texturing

If the sheets of clay produced by these methods are examined carefully some interesting and perhaps useful features will be apparent. The clay, if rolled on hessian, will show the fabric texture. Any dents on the rolling-pin will be reproduced in the clay. The wire cutter drawn through the coarse clay will drag small particles with the wire, revealing yet another texture. If the wire is bent or twisted it will leave score marks across the cut face, tracing the path the wire has taken. Perhaps the wire has slipped and produced a very thinned edge and in places even cut through the sheet leaving an irregular, crumbling, wafer-thin edge. These surfaces and edges may be worthy of preservation for their decorative value which can be effectively incorporated into the finished object. Such incidental features may point the way to further development! If

Fig. 32 A sheet of clay showing the texture of the vegetable sack on which it was rolled

Fig. 33 A clay sheet cut from a perforated block with a piece of knotted string drawn through the clay in see-saw fashion. Note the wooden guide slats

a bent or twisted wire produces an interesting surface, a knotted wire will produce a stronger texture, and if the wire is drawn see-saw through the clay the result will be even more exciting. A carved candle, a chair leg or a square-sectioned piece of wood used as a roller will enrich the surface. Clay rolled out on the threadbare remains of an old carpet, an onion sack or a sheet of corrugated cardboard will gain interesting surface textures. The range of such textures is capable of limitless development but in the final analysis they must be used sensitively in a suitable context.

Building with sheet clay
There are three fundamentally different ways in which the prepared sheets of clay can now be used.

Fig. 34 Textured sheet-clay form made by rolling clay on an opened-out corrugated box

1. Whilst the clay is still soft it can be shaped in such a manner that it is entirely self-supporting. The softness of the clay, its mechanical strength and thickness will all affect its supportive ability. The limited range of possible forms is compensated by the direct and fresh manner in which the clay may be shaped and joined whilst soft.

2. Whilst the clay is still soft it can be formed in, over or around some form of support and left to dry until it is firm enough to become self-supporting. Traditionally, plaster moulds are used because they have soft contours into or over which the clay sheet can be laid and pressed into shape, but there are many other suitable means of support which could be effectively used. Basically, the support should be semi-absorbent so that the clay will not stick to it and split as it dries. The support must also allow the clay to contract as it dries which presents problems if the clay is formed around rather than within a support. Careful judgement is necessary in this instance and the clay must be released from the support as soon as it is sufficiently dry to support itself and before it tightens too firmly on to the former. The same onion sack on which the clay has been rolled out could make a very convenient support if it is suspended hammock-fashion. Gather the opposite edges of the sack with the clay still in position and shake it gently so that the clay assumes the gently swept hammock shape, then tie or pin the sack ends to a suitable support where it can remain until the clay has stiffened. Sand poured into a soft mound also makes a good former over which the clay can be gently draped. The sand will allow the clay to move as it contracts and stiffens. Bricks, wood offcuts, drainpipes and cardboard cylinders of all shapes and sizes make very good formers, but it is generally advisable to place a damp paper hand-towel or tissue between the clay and the former so that the supporting core can be easily removed before the clay shrinks around it. Sharp-edged, angular formers should be used with care because short clays in particular will tend to crack if bent through abrupt angles. They will need to be coaxed and compressed cautiously and gently round such forms. All joined edges should be scratched and slipped before they are worked firmly together. Footballs, tennis balls, polystyrene packing, stiffened hats and many other round objects will provide very useful formers or supports which can be used directly or cast in plaster for use as press moulds.

3. The clay sheet can be formed to the required shape and then left to stiffen before it is joined together in sectional manner. Quite large and complicated structures can be made by this method but discretion and careful judgement must be exercised to prevent the form assuming a rather stiff, lifeless, wooden appearance. The stiffened sections will join quite easily if the surfaces are roughened and coated with slip, but the moisture content of the joined sections must be approximately the same so that they will contract equally as drying shrinkage occurs.

*Fig. 35 Exploring alter-
native methods of making a
perforated and textured clay
sheet*

*Fig. 36 Hammock forming a
sheet of clay. This can be hung
up to stiffen, after which feet
can be grafted on and the form
can be modified by carving, etc*

Fig. 37   A sand mould with sand-formed dishes. The sand will hold its shape better if slightly damp

Fig. 38   A sheet-clay cylinder formed round a rolling-pin. Note the paper hand-towel wrapped round the rolling-pin; this prevents the clay sticking to the wood

Fig. 39 *A plaster cast of a child's plastic ball. Plaster will next be poured over the exposed half of the ball, to the same thickness as the cast portion. The exposed face of the mould has been painted with slip to prevent the two halves sticking together. Note the small registration notch on the mould rim*

1

Fig. 40 *Stages of plaster casting a plastic ball:*
(1) Flatten a rolled length of clay into a flat strip and cut the edges square. Fix the clay strip around the circumference of the ball, keeping at least one face of the clay strip as smooth as possible. The depth of the strip will represent the thickness of the cast. The moisture in the clay will help it stick to the ball but a reinforcing strip may be applied to strengthen the attachment. Ensure that the smooth face is at right angles to the diameter.

2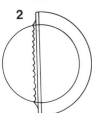

(2) Pour the required amount of water into a plastic bowl and, with dry hands, sprinkle the plaster gently into the water until a small peak of plaster rises above the surface. Allow the plaster to soak for about one minute, then stir gently to a smooth liquid of thin cream consistency. Wait until the plaster shows the first signs of thickening (2–3 minutes), then pour a thin layer of plaster over one half of the ball and the smooth face of the clay wall. This wall will make even contact with the surface to be cast. When the plaster has thickened a little more, build up the thickness of the cast to the depth of the wall over one half of the ball. Leave the plaster to harden (about 10 minutes) and scrape away any that has flowed over the top edge of the clay wall. Now remove the wall and any clay that may still be stuck to the ball, and cut one or two notches in the outside edge of the cast—these will later enable you to register the two halves of the cast. Paint the flat face of the cast with smooth clay slip to prevent the two halves of the mould sticking to each other.

3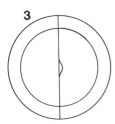

(3) Now repeat the procedure with the exposed half of the ball, using the already cast section with its slipped face as a guide to thickness. As the second half stiffens, scrape away any plaster which has run on to the first half and scrape round the join until you can see the fine line of slip separating the two sections.

4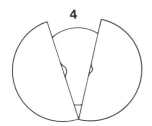

(4) When the mould has hardened (10–12 minutes), run the cast under a tap, applying gentle pressure to separate the two halves of the mould. Remove the ball and leave the mould to dry out before use

39

These three basic methods may be used quite separately or in any appropriate combination. Some forms will be more effective if constructed with very thick, coarse slabs whereas other forms may need fine clay worked to the limit of thinness. Additional clay can be welded on to form feet, lugs, handles or other embellishments, and rims and edges may be thinned by pinching or scraping. Sometimes it is advisable to re-examine traditional methods; you will either arrive at a much more meaningful understanding of just why and how traditional methods have developed or you may produce something which has a sparkle of freshness and originality which flies in the face of the conventional approach. For example, as mentioned above, most traditional press moulds are made with softly curving profiles so that the clay sheet will feed smoothly into position, but if the supporting form is so steep sided that it causes the clay sheet to fold as it is fed into position the folding may be accepted for its intrinsic quality which could enhance the form. Alternatively, the clay may be torn into smaller pieces and pressed into position, patchwork fashion. The inside will need to be welded firmly and smoothed together but the outside may gain decoratively from its patchwork surface. Perhaps the clay block could be deeply punctured so that slices cut from it with the wire could be interestingly perforated. Perhaps the clay slabs could be formed by laying strips of clay into a lattice which could then be rolled firmly together, producing perforated slabs of different character. There are so many ways of forming and decorating with clay slabs that it is impossible to describe all the variations and combinations, and in any case to do so would remove the fun and challenge to individual inventiveness, imagination and judgement.

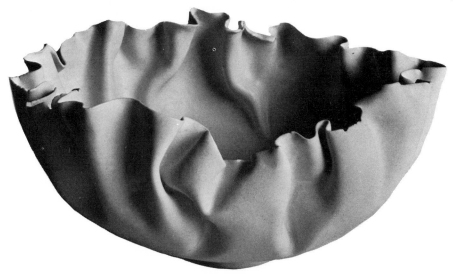

Fig. 41 Convoluted bowl in porcelain by Mary Rogers. This is an example of work with a porcelain-clay sheet. The clay is supported in any suitable former—a basin, bowl, etc.—and small pieces of damp sponge are inserted between the clay and the former to keep the clay in a workable condition. The folds are further pronounced and thinned by pinching the soft clay and later they are thinned again by scraping with a razor blade. Photograph by Eric Webster

40

Fig. 42 A 'patchwork' bowl
is built with torn sheets of
coarse, gritty clay supported in
a colander. This method is
very appropriate to the deep
shape of the former and the
character of the clay

Fig. 43 *A Samian ware bowl 1st century A.D. The form and decoration show close parallels with metal vessels of the same period.* By kind permission of the University Museum of Archaeology and Ethnology, Cambridge

A long step in time from the prehistoric period to the Romans shows some interesting and significant contrasts. By this time man had firmly established a large measure of control over his environment. The small scattered prehistoric settlements had been replaced by densely populated communities. Division of labour was a natural consequence of community living. Farmers provided the food, soldiers defended the community, doctors tended the sick, masons and carpenters built houses. There were musicians, poets and politicians, bakers, wine makers, wheelwrights, smiths and jewellery makers. From centurion to servant, each had his contribution to make within the community structure. Numbered amongst the artists and artisans were the potters who made a wide variety of articles ranging from elegant and refined vases to wine bottles and common domestic ware. The potter's wheel had become a necessity as a means of speeding up production. Fired clay moulds were also used to raise output in what had become a competitive commercial market. For those who could afford them, metal vessels, utensils and containers were an attractive alternative. They had the advantage of durability and serviceability, they were non-porous and, unlike the unglazed pottery of this period, vessels made from the noble metals conferred a mark of social distinction upon their owners. The wheel-thrown products of the period strongly reflect the competition with metal since many of the pottery forms have a rigidity and precision simulating metal rather than clay. Indeed, the highly refined and ornate Samian moulded ware draws very close parallels with metal vessels of the period. It was probably cheapness and speed of production that mainly contributed to the healthy survival of pottery at this time.

Wheel throwing as a method of production required different characteristics of the clay. The coarse, gritty clay used by prehistoric man would have been quite impossible to throw; it would have torn the thrower's hands and would have lacked sufficient plasticity to be drawn into shape on the wheel. The Romans needed a fine smooth clay with good qualities of plasticity. Some naturally occurring clays would have met these requirements, but some clay refining processes were necessary. Coarser clays were probably mixed to a fluid state with water and allowed to settle. The finer particles, remaining in suspension long after the coarse particles had settled, could thus be poured off and dried to the required plastic state for throwing. To speed up the process the fluid clay may have been passed through fine sieves to remove the coarser particles. The Romans were also very skilled at producing ultra-fine clays such as those used for slipping the Samian wares; this clay would have been too sticky for throwing without a proportion of reasonably fine coarse material to give support to the thrown form.

Other technological advances had been made by this time. Not least was the improved method of firing the products. The open firings of prehistoric times were exceptionally wasteful of heat; probably as much as eighty to ninety per cent of heat was lost to the atmosphere and no matter how big the fire or how long it lasted the maximum temperatures achieved would always have been comparatively low. It was necessary to devise some means of delaying the escaping heat so that it was more effectively applied to the pots being fired. The kilns used by the Romans consisted basically of a clay-domed enclosure in which the pots were stacked one upon another. Wood was burned in a connnecting firebox and the flames were drawn from the fire, beneath the floor of the domed chamber, up through the pots and out through a hole at the top of the dome. In this manner the escaping heat was delayed and circulated amongst the pots.

This in principle is an 'up-draught' system which utilizes the natural tendency for heat to rise. As the hot air rises through the kiln and is replaced by air drawn in through the firebox a current or draught of air is established. The speed of the draught through the kiln is regulated by the size of the firebox opening, the size of the hole at the top of the dome and the strength of the heat being produced in the firebox (the fire is of course dependent upon the air supply reaching it). The temperatures achieved in such kilns were not dramatically superior to those achieved by open-firing methods. A gain of about 200–300°C was probable but the principal advantages were a greater refinement of heat control and a considerable saving of fuel. The products were obviously stronger and the firing was cleaner which allowed a wider range of decorative techniques to be used. The contrasts between dark and light fired clays were now used to advantage in decorative processes (see chapter 6). It was fortunate that the thermal shock problem had been solved to a large extent by careful firing management because the gritty, open clays used by prehistoric man to overcome the problem would have been entirely unsuitable for throwing. Indeed it says much for the Roman firing methods that they were able to use fine-textured throwing clays without heavy thermal shock breakages.

CASE HISTORY 5:
Roman pottery in the back garden

We decided to build our own Roman kiln in the back garden. The distribution of local clay is somewhat irregular and although there was no clay in our own garden we discovered that just about a quarter of a mile away some really plastic light grey clay was being excavated on a building site. Two or three journeys with a couple of tea-chests in the back of the car provided enough clay for our purpose. It was very smooth, fine-grained and of considerable plasticity; the finger-ring test showed only very slight, superficial cracks which indicated a good throwing clay.

Some of the clay was immediately heaped into an old tin bath and saturated with water. We poked and stirred it from time to time during the next day or two and it quickly broke down into a fluid mixture which we

Fig. 44   Refining local clay. The crude clay is broken down into a fluid state by adding excess water and alternate soaking and stirring. Natural weathering would achieve the same result but takes more time. The 'slurry' (lumpy clay fluid) is sieved through an 80-mesh sieve and then dried to a suitable consistency

Fig. 45   Roman kiln pit and trench being lined with clay

Fig. 46   Roman kiln. Roofing over the firebox

45

sieved through an eighty mesh phosphor-bronze sieve using a nail-brush. We then allowed the clay to settle and poured off as much water as we could. Having no suitably large absorbent surface on which to dry the clay to workable consistency, we spread out a large plastic sheet on the lawn and poured the sieved clay into a thin layer on it. The warm summer sun soon dried it sufficiently for us to use.

Had we not been so impatient we could have left the clay to weather in the sun, rain and frost which would have saved much labour. We could then have added much more water, making a much thinner slip which could have been sieved through a double layer of nylon stocking or similar fine material after the heavier particles had settled.

Whilst the clay was being refined we started building the kiln. Within an hour we had dug out a circular pit about 18 inches deep and 36 inches in diameter and, at right angles to the pit, a trench 24 inches wide, 48 inches long and 18 inches deep. The pit and trench were then lined throughout with about 5 or 6 inches of clay we had fetched from the building site. This was rammed down very hard. The circle was trued by using an old cycle tyre as a pattern. We then embedded some bars of iron in the clay across the trench about 4 inches above the floor; these were later to act as fire bars. A clay arch was built over the trench and pieces of broken brick, pottery, flowerpots, etc. were beaten in with the clay to strengthen it. The top of the arch inside was brought approximately to ground level, and the arch itself was about 5 inches thick.

Next we pounded clay into an old metal bin and turned the resulting form into the middle of the pit to act as a central support for the perforated floor slabs. Later we became anxious that this support might collapse during firing so we replaced it with ordinary bricks—a slight compromise from the Roman original. The bricks were stood on end on the pit floor and other bricks were balanced horizontally on them to form a fairly loose floor chequer, the top of which was at ground level (and level with the top of the firebox interior arch). The chequer was made closer in the region of the firebox entry. The purified and prepared clay was used to make a kiln load of pots. For speed most pots were thrown on the wheel. The clay threw very well, but before we had made enough pots to fill the kiln it was all used up so we used some of the clay just as it was when dug. Apart from the occasional annoying small stone or hard lump it threw very well. By the next day the pots were dry enough to fire so we built them into a pile on the brick chequer positioned above the circular pit. Care was taken to distribute the weight evenly as one pot was stood on another. They were mainly placed rim to rim or base to base. Small pots were stood inside larger ones but not so that they fitted tightly into each other because they might have tightened on each other and cracked. The circular pit wall was then built up into a dome which covered the pile of pots. As the wads of clay were added to the wall they were laid *across* the five-inch thickness of the wall for strength. Had they been

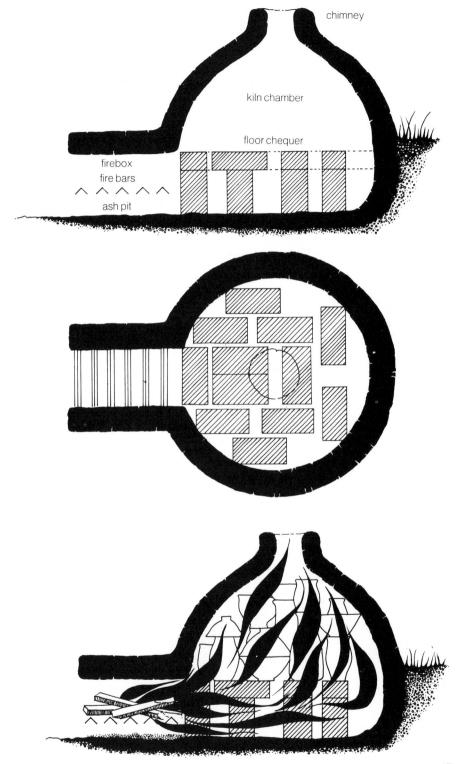

Fig. 47 Diagram of a wood-fired Roman kiln

chimney

kiln chamber

floor chequer

firebox

fire bars

ash pit

47

added to the interior or exterior clay wall face there was the danger that they might have flaked off as the heat dried the wall and caused it to shrink and crack. An opening, about eight to nine inches in diameter was left at the summit of the dome and extended into a short chimney.

The firing began just before eight o'clock the next morning. At first just a few slithers of wood were poked into the firebox and set alight. Smoke slowly issued from the chimney but the fire was too low to feel any warmth yet. A very small but steady supply of wood was fed into the firebox—more smoke and then steam issued from the chimney. Whilst having breakfast the fire went out and we had to start slowly again, having lost some time! Although 'a watched pot never boils' it is never safe to leave a wood-fired kiln for long. Gradually the fire was built up until it was blazing quite merrily by midday. The interior of the kiln was well dried by now and there was considerable dry warmth issuing from the chimney. There was only occasional smoke when the fire was stoked too heavily; at all times it is advisable to feed a wood fire steadily and regularly. Sudden bursts of heavy stoking only deaden the fire and cause irregular heating. The fire was being pulled vigorously from the firebox into the kiln chamber. Previously the flame had hung back in the firebox so the top third of the firebox mouth was covered with a sheet of metal to improve the draw, but now the kiln had dried out and warmed up and a vigorous draught was established. Wood immediately burst into flame as it was fed into the firebox and an oblique cautious glimpse down the chimney showed a dull orange glow within the firebox side of the kiln chamber. The opposite side of the chamber was still black.

Stoking was slowly increased and flames licked out of the chimney. The outside clay surface of the kiln was steaming from the numerous cracks which had appeared. Some cracks were filled with fresh clay but they did not give any real cause for concern. The firebox side of the kiln chamber was red now but still the opposite side was black. We had obviously made an error of judgement with our floor chequer and kiln packing which was allowing too much heat to sweep straight up from the firebox to the dome roof and out through the chimney. It was now too late to alter the chequer but the distribution of heat in the kiln chamber was too uneven. We decided to bore a hole into the back of the kiln chamber and make a second chimney further back. The kiln wall was still soft on the outside. It gradually became warmer as we dug cautiously into it. We made the second chimney hole about four to five inches in diameter. The fire-hardened inner lining of clay rattled down into the kiln as we gave a last push with a long stick and immediately smoke came pouring out of the hole. We laid a roofing tile partly across the original chimney and to our satisfaction saw the flames drawing between the support bricks towards the new 'chimney' we had just made.

By 3.30 p.m. the whole kiln chamber was glowing a bright orange red. The pots were the same colour too and we estimated the heat to be about 1000°C.

The support bricks nearest the firebox looked considerably hotter! We gave a last wood stoking and then sealed up the firebox mouth with the metal sheet and clay. The rear chimney was closed and sealed. The latter stages of the firing had been so clean and smoke-free that we thought the pots might be rather uninteresting in colour. We therefore poured sawdust and bundles of green vegetation down the chimney! (If you try this, beware, because the first applications of sawdust will be thrown back at you in a sheet of flame or shower of sparks.) The chimney was then covered with the tile and sealed with clay to prevent sudden cooling which might possibly have cracked the pots.

The kiln was cool enough to open by mid-morning the next day. We all gathered round in great excitement. The tile was removed from the chimney and we peered in. All looked well. No obvious breakages although the colours were all rather too clean and flat despite our efforts at reduction the day before. We pulled part of the chimney and side of the dome away to remove the pots. Those nearest the firebox were harder fired which we proved by dabbing our tongues on them. The harder pots absorbed the moisture more slowly than the softer pots on the opposite side of the kiln chamber, but all were quite adequately fired. There were a small number of breakages and cracks but these appeared mostly in pots of uneven thickness. Several pots had gone out of shape quite badly. This can happen because of uneven packing but in this case I suspect that the clay was getting near to melting point. The clay we used was Gault clay which has a very high lime content; this probably limited the firing range. The bowls had a good clear ring to them and where we had dipped the pots in a thin slip of red London clay they had fired to a warm toasted brown.

We all agreed that it had been a most enjoyable experience. We were confident that the high temperature (1000°C) and the clean atmosphere of the kiln would have made it possible to glaze-fire in this kiln—a future challenge. Apart from the uneven distribution of heat owing to the error with the floor chequer, the kiln worked very well, but if you want to try making your own Roman kiln don't be tempted to follow these details slavishly to the last inch. That degree of accuracy is not essential. In any case, we used the kiln quite flexibly, sometimes closing the firebox mouth a little, sometimes dampering the chimney. We even made a second chimney outlet as the firing progressed. Remember the basic principle that heat rises. If you stop it rising, which way will it travel? The supply of air to the firebox and the escape of gases from the chimney will be regulated by the size and position of these apertures. If in doubt make them larger because they can more easily be closed than opened. If flame hangs back in the firebox (or even flows forward out of the firebox) then open the chimney to increase the through draught. Much of the process is trial and error so don't be afraid of making mistakes so long as you learn from them.

Opening the Roman kiln— part of the chimney and side of the dome pulled away to remove the pots

Samian ware

If you find the highly polished, almost glaze-like surface quality of the Samian wares attractive you may be interested to see if you can reproduce this surface quality. Basically this is a self-glossing, ultra-fine, red clay slip which has been applied to the moulded form and partially fused, imparting a certain degree of watertightness. It is not understood exactly how the Romans produced such a refined slip but you will be able to achieve similar results by adding a small quantity of Calgon water softener to a fine clay slip. One tablespoon of Calgon added to one pint of red earthenware slip will cause the coarser particles of clay to drop from the slip leaving an ultra-fine mixture which can be carefully syphoned off without disturbing the coarse sediment. This slip can then be applied to leather-hard wares by the usual methods of dipping, pouring, brushing, etc.

Calgon water softener produces this effect because it dissolves the calcium, iron and magnesium compounds present in clay into a complex soluble compound which stays dissolved in the water and assists the 'peptisized' slip to flux (melt) in the firing, producing a light gloss. This approaches a glaze but does not contain enough flux ingredient to achieve a full melt at these temperatures.

Pots treated with this slip and fired in the Roman kiln (or any other kiln) to about 1000°C will produce a rich variety of colours from red to black according to the thickness of the slip and the kiln atmosphere (smoky or clean). Colouring oxides could also be added to the slip to extend the colour range (see chapter 7).

Note: Not all clays have the right structure or composition to react favourably to this treatment. Results cannot be predicted without careful testing.

5 Low-temperature glazed pottery

The great majority of pottery produced today is glazed, that is to say, covered with a layer of glassy material which seals the surface of the object, rendering it non-absorbent. This has very obvious practical advantages and it offers the opportunity to expand the range of surface decoration and colour, but these are opportunities which must be used with reserve and caution. The most beautiful glazes will not disguise a badly or insensitively made object, just as a brilliant and harsh glaze can so easily destroy the beauty of a reserved and sensitive object. There are plenty of monumental failures which underline the need for caution and consideration. The aim should be to achieve a sympathetic harmony between the glaze and the form to which it is applied.

The earliest known examples of glazes were produced in Egypt more than five thousand years ago but, as with most other developments in pottery, progress did not follow a pattern of steady development from this time onwards. Even today there are primitive societies still producing beautiful unglazed pottery which is quite satisfactory for their needs. Development has been influenced by a variety of factors such as the availability of suitable glaze materials and the means of producing temperatures high enough to melt glaze mixtures. In recent times science has unravelled many of the mysteries of glazing and placed our understanding of this complex subject on a much more secure footing, but the exquisite Chinese glazes of some one thousand years ago will probably never be surpassed. The success of the Chinese potters was not based on scientific understanding nor on fortunate guesswork. It was much more the consequence of curiosity, accurate observation, intelligent interpretation of results and attention to detail. These are as much the essential ingredients of success today as they were one thousand years ago.

Low temperature is a comparative term which, in this instance, means somewhere between 800°C and 1100°C. The main body of pottery which comes within this firing range is earthenware, but we will begin by exploring raku, which is a very interesting form of pottery also included within the lower limits of the temperature range. In fundamental principle raku and earthenware are very similar but there are some significant differences. Raku firings, besides being exciting and good fun, are very enlightening. You will be much more forcibly aware of pottery as a product of clay *and fire* as you draw red-hot pots from the kiln. You will also recognize that glaze is not an inert material as you watch it melt, boil and settle smoothly on to the pot. There can be few better ways of gaining a vital and direct involvement with the process of pottery.

Raku

In the traditional raku process the pots are first biscuit fired—that is from dry, raw stage to about 800–900°C—and allowed to cool. The glazes and decoration can then be applied and the pots are placed directly in a red-hot kiln with long-handled tongs. Within a short time, ten to twenty minutes, the glazes will have satisfactorily melted and the pots are then withdrawn with the tongs. Sometimes they are quenched in water and/or smothered in peat, sawdust etc. to smoke-treat them, thus affecting the colours developed. This process introduces certain new considerations.

Kilns and fuels

For raku a kiln is required which will burn fairly cleanly and be capable of reaching and maintaining temperatures of up to 1000°C so that the glazes are adequately melted. The fuels which produce this sort of heat are wood, oil, coal, bottled gas, coke or electricity, but not all of these fuels will burn effectively in the same type of kiln. Electric elements and coke fires give a glowing heat which is transmitted over short distances by radiation and conduction, so the heating elements or coke will need to be placed in the immediate vicinity of the pottery. The other fuels, namely wood, oil, coal and gas, produce long flames and transmit their heat by convection and conduction over quite considerable distances. They will require a combustion area and carefully designed flame routes through the kiln. Wood and coal will require ventilated hearths which the fuels will occupy whilst burning. Careful consideration will need to be given to the supply of air, which will ventilate the fire, providing oxygen for combustion. The kilns using long-flame fuels will require a chimney of suitable proportions to draw the flames through the kiln, but the most effective kilns are those designed in such manner that the flames are delayed within the kiln to give maximum heat effectiveness. This is a question of delicately balanced flame routing and ventilation. A choked fire will be unable to burn effectively and an over-ventilated fire will lose most of the heat up the chimney. Some kilns may be designed for firing with different fuels at different stages of the firing. Oil-fired kilns are often started with bottled gas or wood until the kiln is sufficiently warmed up for the oil to burn effectively.

Kilns for raku glaze firings should be no bigger than the largest object to be fired in them. This is important since the kiln will be regularly loaded and unloaded every ten to twenty minutes when it is at the required maximum temperature, and there is little that can be done to prevent rapid heat loss during these operations. Perhaps well designed pivoted doors and pre-loaded 'fork-lift' type shelves which can be rapidly exchanged will help, but such devices seem, at least in part, to defeat the basic simplicity of the process, and the time taken to satisfactorily fill an unnecessarily large kiln chamber is far too costly in terms of heat lost.

The maximum temperatures required for raku firing (usually up to 1000°C) are still not very high so it would be possible to construct your kiln from a fairly broad range of commonly available materials. Ordinary house bricks are quite suitable, or the kiln could be cast in sections from heat-resistant Ciment Fondu (see suppliers' notes for suitable mixtures). Ordinary jointing cements should *not* be used. Dry-brick jointing is preferable, with a little clay stopping applied to the outside to seal obvious gaps. If you can obtain some pieces of kiln shelving (see list of suppliers), which is made to all sizes from material capable of withstanding frequent heating to high temperatures, they will be very useful for the kiln roof and flooring, but roofing tiles are a possible substitute although they will not survive very high temperatures.

It would be beneficial in the early experimental stages to design your kiln in such a manner that it can be easily modified without major structural changes. It should be possible to close or open the firebox mouth until the air intake is suitably balanced. This is not a 'once and for all' operation but will probably need further regulation as the firing proceeds. The height and diameter of the flue will also modify the speed of draught through the kiln so leave yourself free to experiment here too. A suitably placed flue damper is essential and a few empty tins with tops and bottoms removed can provide adequate flue extensions if needed. It is very much more comfortable if you can arrange to have a side-loading raku kiln because the natural tendency for heat to rise will make it uncomfortable to load and unload the kiln from above. If you open the kiln door a little once the kiln has started to warm up (do not peer over the top of the door and keep your hands and face out of the path of escaping heat) you will probably be able to see the path that the flames are taking. Now watch what happens to the flames if the flue damper is closed gradually. See also what happens to the flames when the firebox mouth is gradually closed. If the kiln door is opened too much while you are looking it will create draughts which will interrupt the normal performance of the flame, but direct observations of the flame path, the speed and colour of the flames, and their reaction to damper adjustments will tell you far more about kilns and firing principles than you can hope to learn from second-hand information.

Although electric kilns have been effectively used by many people for raku firings the procedure cannot be recommended because the associated abrupt heat changes will unquestionably shorten the life of the elements, but perhaps this is a worthwhile risk if no other acceptable facilities are available. If you do use an electric kiln for raku make sure it is fitted with a cut-out switch which operates when the door is opened. *Never* fish inside a live kiln with iron tongs!

To many people who are anxious to attempt an experimental raku firing in the back garden the problem which often arises is how to first biscuit fire the raw pots. The ideal raku kiln is not normally big enough for biscuit firing! There are two possible alternatives. You may make a second enlarged version of the raku kiln which will take enough biscuit ware for your needs or you could make a double-chamber kiln, reserving the small chamber in the hottest part of the kiln for glaze firing, and the larger chamber for biscuit firing. The latter kiln will be a rather more complicated problem for the beginner, and it will involve a long firing cycle since the raw clay pots will need to be fired slowly, as always in the early stages. It will, however, save fuel because the heat will be shared by both chambers. Appropriately placed dampers can be arranged to shut off the biscuit-firing chamber when finished. The biscuited pots can be withdrawn with tongs whilst red hot. They can be cooled, glazed, dried out and glaze-fired straight away.

The illustrated raku kilns are very simple structures which can be erected quickly and at very little cost. The precise dimensions are as much the dictates of practical considerations (such as available brick sizes), as they are of functional necessity. It is not necessary to work slavishly to these dimensions but be aware of general proportions and try to identify the flame pathways. As you gain confidence try your own modifications and improvements.

Clays for raku
It is immediately obvious that the raku firing process subjects the clay to extreme and abrupt heat changes. This is called thermal (heat) shock. The ability of clays to withstand this thermal shock depends on:

1. The chemical composition of the clay. Some of the clay ingredients act as fluxes and will start to melt at fairly low temperatures. The proportion and type of fluxes present will, in part, determine how soon and how much melting takes place. Earthenware clays start melting much sooner than stoneware, porcelain and fireclays because they contain a much higher proportion of fluxes. A certain degree of melting is essential to the fired strength of the clay object

but too much will make it too rigid to give to the stresses of sudden heating.

2. The physical composition of the clay. Clay ingredients of very small particle size have relatively greater surface areas at which chemical reaction takes place. The thinned, flattened, sheetlike structure of clay particles further increases the surface area for more rapid and complete chemical reaction. The rounded and more angular refractory (heat-resistant) clay ingredients (sand, flint, grog, etc.) reduce the speed of chemical reaction, raise the melting point and open the clay, imparting more 'elasticity' to the fired clay.

3. The temperature to which the clay is fired. The melting of the clay is progressively more complete as the firing temperature is raised. Sintering (point-to-point fusion) is the first stage of melting, leading ultimately to vitrification. A vitrified clay is very dense, non-absorbent, and has considerable rigid strength. It is usual to biscuit fire below the vitrification point so that glazes may be easily applied.

The rigid strength of a well vitrified clay body does not respond well to abrupt thermal shock. The best clay bodies for raku are those which are low in body flux, coarse and/or angular in particle size and shape, and which have been biscuit fired at a low temperature (800–900°C). A suitable basis for such a body is a coarse fireclay or stoneware clay opened with additions of sand or flint. Your local clay deposits will probably be suitable for raku firing if they are opened with a liberal amount of sand (about one-third sand to two-thirds clay). It is almost certain that all the red firing clays will need this same treatment. The visual appearance of your clay is no clear guide to how it will perform during firing; accurate assessment can be made only by trying it. If it shatters due to thermal shock do not give up until you have tried tempering it with further additions of sand, flint and grog (fired and ground clay). It may also make a useful blend when mixed with other refractory (high-firing) clays, such as stoneware, fireclay and porcelain. The major craft pottery suppliers usually offer clays suitable for raku if you cannot succeed with your own local clay.

In contrast to the traditionally very coarse, rugged clays used for raku it is interesting to note that it is possible to use a porcelain clay such as Podmore's P.1035. This is a relatively expensive clay but very interesting to work with because of its very smooth texture and whiteness. It probably succeeds as a raku clay because it has a low clay content and the additional body ingredients have a more angular particle shape. It would be an under-fired and therefore low-vitrified body at raku temperatures.

Most raku clays are too rugged to throw but they are very suitable for coiling, pinching, slab-building etc. All clay joints must be made with meticulous care because the thermal shock will expose any weakness.

Raku glazes

The temperature range for raku glazes is normally between 850°C and 950°C. Within this temperature range the glaze ingredients must melt and they normally form a smooth, glassy, secure coating. This is a very low temperature for glazes and the range of materials which will perform satisfactorily is somewhat limited. Lead and/or borax are the most important fluxes (melting agents) used in the glazes at this temperature. Both lead and borax are soluble in most natural forms (except borax in the form of colemanite) and must therefore be used in fritted form (pre-melted together with other materials—particularly silica—and thus rendered insoluble). The frits are supplied in finely-ground powdered form. Soluble materials used in glazes will become solvent in the water used to mix the glazes and will be absorbed into the porous biscuited ware when the glaze is applied. They will also crystallize out at the glaze surface as the water evaporates, producing a disturbance in the distribution of glaze ingredients. *It is important to note that unfritted, soluble lead is very poisonous and may not be used in schools.*

An essential ingredient of all pottery glazes is silica. This material melts at just over 1700°C forming a clear glass when cooled. Unfortunately clay would also collapse and melt completely at this temperature so silica alone cannot be used as a glaze for pottery. There is, however, a small range of other materials (known as fluxes) which can be added to silica and which will cause it to melt at much lower temperatures within acceptable limits to be used as a glaze on pottery.

The best starting point for making raku glazes is with a commercially prepared low-temperature (low melting point) frit since the problems of solubility and toxicity are then largely avoided. Within the raku-glaze firing range (850–1000°C) there are three principally different frits which could be used:

1. The lead frits:
   lead monosilicate—melts at 750–950°C,
   lead sesquisilicate—melts at 800–1050°C,
   Lead bisilicate—melts at 900–1100°C.
   These are principally compounds of lead and silica. Lead monosilicate contains the most lead and least silica and melts at a lower temperature than lead sesquisilicate which, for the same reason, melts at a lower temperature than lead bisilicate.
2. The borax frits. These frits vary in composition from one manufacturer to another but always contain silica and borax together with other fluxes.
3. The alkaline frits. These frits also vary in composition. They contain silica and often borax also but derive their name from the alkalis (sodium and potassium) which are used to flux (melt) the silica.

Most suppliers today give brief notes in their catalogues about the frits which they supply. These merit careful attention when you are choosing which frit to use. Especially note the temperature ranges quoted and select those frits which have the lowest temperature range. One frit from each of the three groups will give sufficient variety for a good range of glazing experimentation.

These frits would in fact perform as raku glazes on their own but it is usually necessary to make small additions of a few other materials for various reasons.

1. To help the glaze stick on the pot before and during firing:
   bentonite 1–4%,
   or clay 5–10%,
   or plain flour 5%,
   or various gums.
2. To raise the firing temperature:
   flint 10–15%,
   or clay 5–15%,
   or feldspar 10–20%.
3. To reduce the fluidity of the glaze:
   clay 5–15%,
   feldspar 10–20%.
4. To prevent the glaze settling:
   clay 5–10%,
   bentonite 1–4%.
5. To make the glaze white and opaque when fired:
   tin oxide 5–8%,
   zirconium 8–12%.
6. To colour the glaze:
   copper oxide 2–4%,
   cobalt oxide $\frac{1}{4}$–1%,
   manganese dioxide 2–4%,
   iron oxide 2–8%.

Finely ground rust scales, verdigris, Bordeaux mixture (a tomato fungicide containing copper) and iron-enriched plant preparations obtainable from horticultural shops will prove very interesting for experimental purposes. It will be noted that some materials mentioned serve more than one function. Additions of clay will improve the suspension of the glaze, will help the raw glaze to stick on the pot, will make the fired glaze less runny and will generally raise the temperature at which the glaze will melt. Almost any bottle glass, including coloured glasses, will make glazes if they are crushed to a fine powder and mixed with a little clay. A pestle and mortar is the best means of crushing glass. If such is available put the lumps of glass in the mortar then put the pestle handle first into the toe of an old stocking and stretch the wider part of the stocking leg over the mouth of the mortar. This will overcome the danger of flying glass splinters whilst enabling you to see what is happening to the glass. Windscreen glass can also be used and this has the advantage that it does not splinter dangerously like bottle or window glass. You can also buy 'Cullett' which is ready crushed glass. The finer the glass is powdered, the easier it will be to apply when mixed with water and a little clay and it will melt and react much quicker too. In fact, finely powdered glass is very similar in some respects to finely powdered frits.

There are very comprehensive books devoted entirely to the subject of glazes, which is really a very complex and involved science of ceramics, but perfectly acceptable results can be obtained with a minimum of knowledge. It is advisable to keep the glaze mixtures as simple as possible to start with. The frits will normally provide 80 to 90 per cent of a raku or low-temperature glaze. Clay may be the only other necessary ingredient. Any other ingredients should be introduced and tested one at a time so that you can see clearly how they affect the glaze.

Line Blends are a very quick and effective method of testing glazes. For this you will need a strip of biscuit-fired raku clay tile divided into several sections. Suppose you want to find out exactly how much clay you need to add to a particular frit to make a suitable basic raku glaze. We know that the frit is almost satisfactory as a glaze by itself so the amount of clay added will not be very great. If you make up two glazes at either extreme of the likely range then, by blending them together in varying progressive proportions, you can hope to find the right balance, e.g.:

glaze A   7 teaspoonfuls frit
                3 teaspoonfuls clay
glaze B 10 teaspoonfuls frit

Now add sufficient water to both glazes to bring them to the consistency of evaporated milk and sieve them through a fine sieve (eighty mesh preferably). When this has been done bring both glazes to exactly the same volume by making up the difference with water; if the glazes are mixed in identical plastic cream tubs, or something similar, and stood side by side, it is an easy matter to bring them to the same level if you do not have a graduated fluid measure. They can now be blended, in level teaspoonful measures stirred together in another mixing cup, and then applied to the test tile thus:

all A   5   4   3   2   1   teaspoonfuls A

          1   2   3   4   5   all B   teaspoonfuls B

The ratios of these mixtures will simplify thus: $5:1; 2:1; 1:1; 1:2; 1:5$, and if the simplified ratios are used you will save on glaze.

For simplicity of calculation the number of 'steps' in the blending process should be decided according to the following:

1. The difference between the maximum and minimum ends of the scale:

    Mixture A contains 3 teaspoonfuls clay, and 7 teaspoonfuls frit.

    Mixture B contains 0 teaspoonfuls clay, and 10 teaspoonsful frit.

The range is therefore 3–0 clay; 7–10 frit.

The above test will represent:

3	2½	2	1½	½	0	parts of clay
7	7½	8	8½	9½	10	parts of frit

i.e. decreasing by half a part of clay and increasing by half a part of frit at each blend.

2. The refinement of testing. Decreasings of one part each would necessitate a four-step blend:

teaspoonfuls A	all A	2	1	0	=	3	2	1	0	clay
teaspoonfuls B	0	1	2	all B	=	7	8	9	10	frit

Decreasings of a quarter of a part each would necessitate a thirteen-step blend:

all A	11	10	9	8	7	6	5	4	3	2	1	0	teaspoonfuls
0	1	2	3	4	5	6	7	8	9	10	11	all B	
		5:1	3:1	2:1		1:1		1:2	1:3	1:5			simplified ratios
3	2¾	2½	2¼	2	1¾	1½	1¼	1	¾	½	¼	0	parts clay
7	7¼	7½	7¾	8	8¼	8½	8¾	9	9¼	9½	9¾	10	parts frit

The choice of refinement depends upon the reactivity of the material being tested. Colouring oxides tested by this system would probably need the finer blend range; whereas clay/frit mixtures would not need such a degree of refinement. It is important to remember that the mixtures must be stirred thoroughly each time before use if an accurate result is to be obtained because the ingredients often settle very quickly. For accurate assessment of results the glazes should be tested on vertical and horizontal surfaces; the vertical surfaces will indicate how runny the glaze is. The glazes are best applied by dipping or pouring from a teaspoon since a smooth, even glaze layer (about one sixteenth of an inch thick) is essential.

Raku glazes tested by this method can be popped into the kiln and within ten to fifteen minutes, or less, the results will be available. Remember to mark the tests carefully on the back of the tile (with iron oxide or other material which will not burn away) for future reference. The results will not only depend on the glaze mixture but also on:

1. The thickness of glaze applied.
2. The heat of the kiln.
3. The time taken to fire the test.
4. The kiln atmosphere (clean or smoky).
5. Post-firing treatments.

There is more than one way to tackle a problem glaze. If the glaze is too runny it may be improved by adding clay or feldspar. Alternatively, it may be improved by firing at a slightly lower temperature. It might also be improved simply by substituting a different clay in the glaze mixture, since clays vary considerably.

Of course, blending materials in this manner takes no account of the weights of the materials, which will often differ widely. The lead frits, for example, are much heavier bulk for bulk than any of the other glaze ingredients mentioned. Should you wish to mix glaze ingredients by weight then you must establish their respective bulk-weight factors. To do this, take a consistent measure (e.g. a level teaspoonful) of each material and weigh it accurately in grams or ounces. The resultant figure will be the bulk-weight factor. Then if the dry measure is multiplied by the bulk-weight factor the result will be the dry-weight ratio, which in turn can be converted to a percentage if required. For example:

	Bulk-weight factor		Dry-weight ratio	%
Frit (8 tablespoonfuls) ×	21·5	=	172	$\frac{172}{204} \times 100 = 84 \cdot 3$
Clay (2 tablespoonfuls) ×	16·0	=	32	$\frac{32}{204} \times 100 = 15 \cdot 7$
		Total	204	

This is an unscientific and inaccurate method of making glazes, but it works very well most of the time and will give you a rich understanding which will provide a good springboard from which to launch into the scientific approach later on if you wish.

Applying the glazes. The glazes can be applied to the biscuit-fired pots by a wide variety of methods. They may be poured on, brushed on or sprayed or the pots can be dipped into them. Coloured clay slips can be applied to the raw pots before biscuit firing to later influence the glazes, or colouring oxides can be mixed with the glazes or painted either under or on to the glaze before glaze firing. There are endless possibilities to be explored.

Glaze firing. Dry the pot thoroughly before putting it into the hot kiln for glaze firing otherwise sudden heating and the sudden formation of steam within the pot walls may cause breakages, even at this stage. Hold the glazed pot securely in a long-handled pair of tongs and place it steadily in the red-hot kiln; a pair of gloves will provide useful protection for your hands. (In the absence of a suitable pair of tongs two long metal rods may be used but with some loss of stability.) Shut the kiln door quickly to avoid too much heat loss. Watch the pot every three to four minutes now and see what happens to the glazes. A built-in spy-hole is useful or you can open the kiln door a fraction to watch what is happening but again, try to avoid too much heat loss. If the kiln is at a good temperature the glazes will soon start to boil. You will see the glaze bubble up like slowly boiling toffee. Soon the bubbles will settle down and the glaze will appear smooth and shiny; the pot is then ready to be brought out with the tongs. The glaze at this point will be soft and sticky. The tongs will leave small scars on the surface but these will partly heal because the glaze is molten. Teamwork is helpful during these operations for quick efficient action. Someone will be needed to operate the kiln door, someone to unload and reload the kiln and perhaps someone else to cover the pots with sawdust.

Post-firing treatments. What happens next is again a matter of choice. The pot may be:

1. Left to cool.
2. Plunged into cold water to develop crazing (fine cracks) in the glaze for decorative effect, although most raku glazes will normally craze without any assistance.
3. Plunged into a bed of sawdust, peat, dry vegetation or any other material that will produce smoke which will reduce the glaze-colouring oxides and darken any exposed clay body.

These processes can be combined, e.g. the pot can be dipped quickly into water and then in sawdust whilst it is still hot enough to burn the sawdust and make smoke for reduction. The glaze can then be partly re-oxidized by removing the pot from the sawdust while it is still very hot. Thus it can be seen that the decisions do not end once the glazes and decoration have been applied. Explore the possibilities and note the outcome of each decision with great care; even the decision to leave the pot in the kiln another minute longer may capture or lose some desirable quality. It may be only one small patch of glaze that will give a vital clue about glaze thickness, temperature, colour etc. A pot can be glaze-fired more than once if necessary, or it can be double glazed if the glaze is thickened (by pouring off some water after the glaze has settled) to adjust for loss of absorbency of the glazed pot. Glazes which are rich in lead tend to blister if heavily reduced, but do not confuse this blistering with that caused by too heavy a use of colouring oxides or an immature glaze. Peat seems to give rise to less blistering than sawdust although

I cannot explain why. Certainly there are many factors to consider and numerous possibilities to explore.

CASE HISTORY 6:
the clay raku kiln

We decided to construct this kiln using, as far as possible, only clay. We smashed the remaining walls of the Roman kiln (see chapter 5) back into the pit and hosed it with water to soften the clay. The interior face of the Roman kiln clay walls had been so strongly heated that the fired clay acted as a useful coarse aggregate to reduce cracking, but crushed bricks, broken tiles or pots etc. would have served the same purpose. For the kiln site we chose a piece of ground with a slight slope on it. We made this into a split level with a 5-inch step which was later to form the back of the firebox. The side walls of the firebox were raised to 3 inches above the level of the step and a 3-inch bed of clay was pounded into place between the walls and up the face of the step. Half a dozen pieces of scrap angle iron were set into the clay from wall to wall to act as fire bars, the space below being the ash pit. The side walls were then continued upwards into a strong arch leaving a 9-inch clearing above the fire bars. The 8-inch thick walls of the kiln chamber were then laid out to form a rectangle 22 inches by 12 inches internally and built up to a level with the firebox arch. We then found a board large enough to build a clay slab 19 inches by 12 inches by 12 inches by 3 inches thick. We rammed the slab together very firmly and trimmed the sides exactly to the required dimensions. Next we built more clay up on the longer outside edges of the slab to about 6 inches and beat this into a concave arch. In the thinner section of the arch we pierced holes about 1 inch in diameter right through the slab. The slab was then turned upside down and dropped into position to form the floor of the kiln chamber. One edge of the slab was welded with clay to the end of the firebox arch, leaving a 3-inch flameway gap at the opposite end. The arched side of the floor slab connected with the arch of the firebox, forming a continuous flame path about 6 inches by 9 inches under the floor of the kiln chamber, which was perforated to allow some heat to pass up through the floor.

The kiln-chamber walls were then raised another 10 inches but a 10-inch door opening was left on one side and three bricks were loosely stood into it. Another gap 10 inches by 3 inches deep was left in the wall directly above the firebox arch; this was to become the entrance to the flue which was built on top of the firebox arch. All the walls were pounded firmly together using heavy blocks of wood, and the clay was used as dry as possible to minimize shrinkage. At this level (10 inches above perforated floor level) two lengths of angle iron from an old bed frame were laid lengthwise along the interior sides of the kiln chamber and built into the end walls. They were spaced so that three roofing tiles would fit loosely across them, forming the floor of the up-

Fig. 48 Firebox and kiln chamber base constructed from local clay

Fig. 49 The perforated clay kiln floor in position. Flames from the firebox will pass under the floor arch and rise to the crown of the kiln through the perforations and rear slot. The rear slot could be enlarged somewhat if a controlling damper were positioned at this point; this particular dimension is a rather critical one which could prove to be difficult to alter in the event of a miscalculation. A roofing tile inserted horizontally in the wall would make an efficient damper

Fig. 51   Diagrams of the all-clay kiln

chimney

10 in.

door

10 in.

roofing-tile shelves

angle-iron shelf supports

6 in.

3 x 10 in.

28 in.

door

22 in.

3 x 10 in.

9 in.

firebox

5 in.

ash pit

6 in.

These are critical dimensions which it might be safer to make larger; an adjustable damper could be fitted as a means of control.

per chamber. The walls were then built upwards and inwards into a dome producing an upper chamber 18 inches deep (to the apex). Another 10-inch square opening was left for access to the upper chamber but, for strength, it was positioned on the opposite side from the doorway to the lower chamber. At the same time the chimney stack was continued upwards almost to the level of the domed roof, and then a drainage pipe 3 feet by 4 inches was used to complete the chimney. The kiln was now ready for use, having taken a day to build without hurrying.

Firing

The same evening we packed both upper and lower chambers with raw clay pots made from various mixtures of prepared and local clays blended with generous helpings of sand or grog. One of the three roofing tiles was removed from the upper chamber floor to encourage free circulation of heat. The two remaining tiles were spaced a little apart to provide adequate support for the load of pots, and the third tile was placed in the ash pit of the firebox so that it would be hot when required later on. The firebox was half-filled with sawdust and set alight; we left it to burn slowly through the night to warm and dry out the kiln and its contents.

By 6.45 a.m. the next morning the sawdust had burned away and we fed in the first few sticks of wood. Gradually, during the morning, the fire was built up, though at first it did not draw into the kiln very well and much steam issued from the chimney. We assumed that the heavy steam in the kiln was making the fire sluggish but the problem persisted even after most of the moisture had been driven off. There was obviously a constriction at some point which was choking the fire. The 4-inch drainage-pipe chimney section looked as if it could be causing trouble so we took it off. The improvement was immediately noticeable but we were still not entirely satisfied so we built the chimney stack up to its original height (approximately 4 feet) using clay slabs and maintaining a 7-inch internal diameter all the way up the flue. This produced the desired effect and by 4.00 p.m. the interior of the kiln was glowing red hot. There was a very even distribution of heat and flames even licked out of the chimney. We removed the brick doors and took out the red-hot pots with long-handled tongs. The shelf tiles were then slid along the angle-iron channels until they fitted tightly to the walls and the third tile was removed from the ash pit and laid into the gap between the other two tiles, thus effectively sealing off the upper chamber.

Long tongues of flame danced through the floor perforations and looped through the lower chamber towards the flue opening. We were soon able to slip our glaze tests into the kiln and within ten minutes we drew them out, red hot with smooth glistening patches of molten glaze on them. At least four of the glazes looked very promising. They were:

> 9 tbsp. powdered blue glass from a
> milk-of-magnesia bottle   *(continued over)*

65

½ tsp. bentonite
1 tbsp SM ball clay

9 tbsp. lead sequisilicate
1 tsp. bentonite
1 tbsp. CY ball clay

8 tbsp. lead bisilicate
1 tsp. bentonite
1 tbsp. CY ball clay

8 tbsp. Podmore's J. frit
1 tsp. bentonite
1 tbsp. CY ball clay

We mixed up about half a pint of each of these four glazes and applied
them to the pots which were quite cool now. We poured, dipped and brushed
the glazes on and painted some with thin brush strokes of Bordeaux mixture
which had been dissolved in water. The pots were stood on and around the
firebox to dry and warm and were then fed, a few at a time, into the lower kiln
chamber. From time to time we peeped cautiously into the kiln and saw the
glazes boiling and bubbling. Within ten minutes the glazes had melted and
matured. The pots were removed with the long tongs and placed into a
bucket of sawdust which burst into flame until smothered with another layer
of sawdust. The kiln was reloaded with more pots and the cycle was repeated
at approximately ten-minute intervals. Some pots were plunged in cold
water, others were just left to cool; a few were rolled in leaves and lawn trimmings. The results were surprisingly good, though the reduced pots were
generally the best. We had to scrub the pots with steel wool to remove the
soot on them and reveal the rich variety of colours. The Bordeaux mixture
produced magnificent colour from gleaming coppery lustres to browns, reds,
greens and turquoise depending on the glaze used, the clay body and the post-
firing treatment (whether reduced or oxidized). The exposed clay body, when

*Fig. 52 After eight hours
firing the biscuit-fired pots
were withdrawn whilst still
red hot. Note that the biscuit
firing is fairly tightly packed
and the pots may be stood on
each other. Flames can be seen
rising through the perforated
floor. Long-handled iron tongs
should be used to remove the
pots*

66

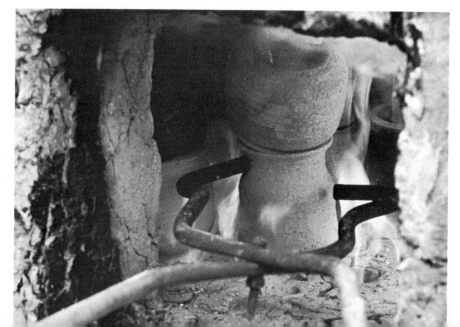

reduced in sawdust, turned black and formed an exciting colour foil to the glazed areas. Where the glazes had crazed, the sawdust smoke penetrated through the glaze to the body etching an exciting network of dark lines. Some of the lead glazes had blistered with too much reduction but the success rate was very high. Glaze 4—the J. frit glaze—had produced a delightful salmon-pink colour at a certain critical temperature. If heated only slightly more it became a pleasant semi-transparent white. The difference in temperature between one side of a pot and the other was enough to lose or gain this fugitive but most attractive colour—a point to note carefully for the future!

Fig. 53 Some pots have already been returned to the kiln for glaze firing while other biscuit-fired pots await decoration and glaze. Large cracks have appeared in the structure but these did not affect the firing. Note the modified chimney

Fig. 54 Two pinch-pot, raku-fired bowls from the all-clay kiln. The craze lines in the glaze were pronounced by embedding the pots in sawdust while they were still red hot

67

Fig. 55 Coke-fired raku kiln displayed. Note the ventilation/rake holes at the base and the open coke-feed hopper at the top. The brickwork has been coated with a layer of fireclay and sawdust for sealing and insulation. A metal sheet will be positioned from the top of the sagger to the top of the door to minimize the risk of coke falling into the sagger

CASE HISTORY 7:
a coke-fired raku kiln

The pots for this firing had previously been biscuit fired so we only needed a small kiln chamber sufficient to glaze-fire two or three pots at a time. The kiln size was also determined by the sagger (an open-sided, box-like shape made from fireclay and able to withstand frequent heating to high temperatures) which we had bought for this purpose. It was 18 inches square and 9 inches deep. We made a level floor of bricks and then stood the sagger on its side supported on two brick piers 6 inches high. An outer brick wall was then built round the sagger leaving a minimum $4\frac{1}{2}$-inch gap between the brick wall and sagger; fire-bricks were used but common building bricks would be suitable. A rake-and-ventilation hole was left at the foot of each of the four walls, at ground level. A loose brick door was left opposite the open sagger mouth and a sheet of metal was laid from the top of the sagger to the wall above the door opening. This was done to prevent coke falling into the open sagger. The last two brick layers were stepped in a little but the top was left open for stoking. The outside walls were plastered with a thin layer of sand and fireclay to reduce heat loss.

A vigorous wood fire was kindled around the empty sagger and coke was fed in from the top. Once the coke was well alight more coke was poured in until it filled the space surrounding the sagger. Within four hours the kiln was hot enough for glaze firing and a glazing cycle of between ten and fifteen minutes was begun. Our biggest pots were no taller than 9 inches so we were continually wasting a lot of kiln space. We tried to arrange a shelf in the sagger but this increased the loading time and resulted in more loss of heat. We achieved excellent firing temperatures and results but our pot sizes did not justify such a large and uneconomic sagger. It is easy enough to make your own saggers from a heavily grogged high-temperature clay (such as that used for raku clay body). They can be slabbed or coiled to shape and biscuit fired and it would be helpful to have two or three sizes to choose from. Roofing tiles can also be used to make a protective enclosure for the pots within the burning coke. On one occasion when we were using roofing tiles they slipped off the supports and collapsed so we just stood one tile on top of the blazing coke heap and fired our pots on that with good results. In fact, if the pot forms have broad stable bases and are unglazed at the bottom they can be stood directly on the burning coke, without a tile.

Coke fires have the advantage that they need less stoking and attention but little flame is produced. The heat is transmitted to the pots by radiation and conduction so the pots must be placed as close to the burning coke as possible. All the usual glazes, decorating processes and techniques and post-firing treatments may be used (as described for the all-clay raku kiln).

CASE HISTORY 8:
an oil-fired raku kiln

This small kiln was made from high-grade insulation bricks which are very expensive, but they do hold the heat in the kiln and therefore save fuel. Common house bricks could just as well be used. The source of heat was a large second-hand G.P.O. oil brazing lamp, like a large blowlamp; a propane-gas burner is a good alternative. The kiln was dry-brick built and a precast Ciment Fondu slab was used to roof over the kiln chamber, although it could have been closed in with stepped brickwork. A piece of kiln shelf (or roofing tile) was raised about 2 inches on kiln shelf props (small pieces of brick could be substituted). Some thick 3-inch iron piping was used for a chimney. The flame was directed into the kiln through a 2-inch square gap in the bricks and ran under the raised floor. The flame hit the back wall and shot upwards, across the roof and out of the chimney. We later modified this design by removing the piece of vertical tile since the flame naturally rose vertically at this point, but we dropped the iron chimney barrel right down to the shelf floor level, made a 3-inch vertical cut across the diameter of the pipe and removed a half-section so that the flue entry was directly above the flame entry point. This produced a more complete circulation of heat with improved performance.

By increasing the height of the kiln with several layers of bricks we found we could increase capacity sufficiently to allow biscuit firings to take place. The size is limited only by the available heat input. Oil or propane burners enable small kilns to be heated rapidly (one and a half to two hours) to glazing temperatures—an important feature if the kiln is to be used within a limited working time. One such kiln was built and fired in a garage; another, fired with propane, was built indoors on a concrete floor; and yet another was used by primary-school children on the back door steps of the school—much to the children's delight. With adequate supervision there are no serious dangers; children have a natural and healthy respect for red-hot kilns and pots. The most dangerous time is when things have partly cooled down and no longer *look* hot.

Obviously the raku kiln you choose must be suitable for your needs, but the choice should also depend upon what materials and equipment you have available, the situation in which it is to be used and, possibly, the length of firing cycle as well.

Egyptian paste

The very first glazes ever produced were probably discovered initially by a lucky accident made possible by a coincidental set of circumstances. Some 7000 years ago in Egypt it was noticed that some clay objects produced a shiny surface when fired. This aroused interest which must have prompted further investigation. What was responsible for this phenomenon? Could anything be done to improve the quality? Was it something in the clay or something about the firing? One can imagine the questions that these people might have asked themselves. It may have been a coincidence of geological features which brought together these minerals but man recognized a new potential in the materials he was using and from this a rather unusual clay body was developed. This is known as Egyptian paste and the word 'paste' describes the material more accurately than the word clay. The clay content is usually very low and this reduces the plasticity of the paste very considerably. It is usually quite unsuitable for throwing. It was used by the Egyptians principally for making beads, trinkets and small models which is understandable in view of the limitation imposed by its very low plasticity. A fairly high percentage of body flux is present to produce sufficient body strength at the low temperature (920–970°C) to which the material is fired.

Fig. 56 A very small oil-fired (brazing lamp) raku kiln displayed to show the under-floor flameway and baffle walls. This kiln could also be fired with a propane torch

Fig. 57 An extended version of the oil-fired raku kiln packed for indoor biscuit firing

Fig. 58 A primary-school child removing a glazed raku pot from the kiln. More pots, glazed and decorated, are drying out on the kiln top in readiness for glaze firing

The ingredient which produces the glaze is a soluble alkali–soda. Soluble materials are not usually of much use in glazes (see page 56) but because the soda is soluble and dissolves in the water of the paste it will migrate with the water to the surface of the object as drying occurs and will be deposited there as a dry crystalline powder. Care is necessary in handling at this stage so that the raw glaze deposit is not disturbed. It will be seen that even drying is essential if an even glaze deposit is required. The high proportion of non-plastic body ingredients (e.g. flint, sand, feldspar etc.) produce a very open body which makes it very much easier for evaporation to occur evenly if the objects are stood in a position where air is able to circulate freely around them.

The forms of soluble soda which are suitable for use in Egyptian paste are sodium carbonate (soda ash) and sodium bicarbonate. The soda forms a glaze principally by combining with the silica of the clay (see page 56) although it seems likely that other body ingredients may be involved to a localized extent at the surface of the clay.

Other Egyptian paste ingredients are:

Ball clay for plasticity.
Flint (300-mesh) to increase the silica with which the soda combines to form the glaze.
Fine sand to open the texture of the clay.
Feldspar or whiting to strengthen the fired paste. These materials are not particularly active at such low temperatures and a good alternative would be a low-temperature alkaline frit.
Bentonite to improve plasticity.

Here are some Egyptian paste recipes:

Ingredient	Parts				
Soda feldspar	35	20	—	—	35
Whiting	5	7	—	—	—
Podmore's Tor J. Frit (or similar)	—	14	28	12	—
Ball clay	26	27	50	35	17
Sodium carbonate (soda ash)	12	5	10	8	10
Sodium bicarbonate	—	5	—	—	3
Flint (300 mesh)	20	25	10	35	35
Fine sand	—	—	—	8	—
Bentonite	2	2	2	2	—

Mixing. The difficulty in preparing this paste is to calculate the water content accurately. If excess water has to be removed the soluble soda salts will be lost with it. The water content will be between 20 and 25 per cent of the total batch weight (depending in part upon the proportion of plastic and non-plastic ingredients). First dissolve the soda in the water and then add the other ingredients (previously mixed dry). Knead the paste thoroughly and use as soon as possible after mixing. Should any delay in use be unavoidable, wrap the paste very lightly in plastic and knead again before using. The paste does not keep well because there is a strong tendency for the soda to crystallize.

Colouring agents should be mixed with the soda in the water, as follows:

Copper carbonate	1–3% (turquoise)
Cobalt oxide	$\frac{1}{4}$–1% (blue)
Manganese dioxide	$\frac{1}{4}$–2% (pink–purple)
Chromic oxide	$\frac{1}{2}$–3% (yellow–green)
Iron oxide	1–10% (pink–salmon-pink)

The colours achieved with Egyptian paste are among its most attractive features, particularly the copper turquoise range. Pastes of contrasting colours can be used in decorative combination, and impression decoration is also effective.

Development. Potassium carbonate (pearl ash) might be worth experimenting with as a part-substitute for the soda.

A very light firing earthenware clay, such as the Gault clay, might make a useful substitute for the ball clay and some of the feldspar and whiting since the Gault clay is much more fusible and plastic.

Washing starch, mixed with boiling water to a thick consistency, can be used as a substitute for bentonite to improve plasticity (up to 8 per cent of total bulk weight).

Firing. Since the objects will be 'glazed' all over they should be placed on stilts or sand to avoid them sticking to the kiln shelves. Temperatures are quite important since even slight overfiring will cause the whole body to boil and blister. Draw-rings are perhaps the best guide to the maturity of the glaze. Beads can be threaded on to old electric-kiln element wires.

Earthenware
Much that has been said about the raku process will apply to earthenware. There are, however, some important differences:

Clay body
Raku　Usually a coarse, open body of refractory ingredients.
　　　Very low vitrification. Weak.
Earthenware　A variable body but often fine and quite dense. High proportion of fusible ingredients.
　　　Fairly well vitrified. Strong.

Biscuit firing
Raku　Low biscuit firing (below 1000°C) to reduce vitrification.

Earthenware   Not necessarily biscuit fired. Often high biscuit fired (1100°C) to reduce crazing of glazes.

Glaze firing
Raku   Placed directly into kiln pre-heated to glaze temperature. Removed immediately glazes have matured.
Earthenware   Full glaze-firing cycle from cold to maximum temperature and back to cool.

Glazes
Raku   Mature at 800–1000°C approx.
Earthenware   Usually mature at approximately 1000–1150°C.

Reduction
Raku   During or immediately after glaze firing.
Earthenware   During firing programme, if at all.

These differences originate from the differences in firing procedures. Raku must be able to withstand the thermal shock of the glaze firing. Earthenware has a much more amenable firing programme, although there are exceptions to these general definitions, such as the flameproof earthenwares. For earthenware the same opportunities, to operate directly on the melted glazes (e.g. reduction procedures) as they cool, do not exist. Earthenware pots must never touch in a glaze firing since the glazes will be solidified before the pots are removed. Only mild glaze disturbance will show if glazed raku pots touch since they will be parted whilst the glazes are still fluid.

Most of the pre-firing shaping, decorating and glazing techniques of raku can be applied to earthenware. Although the same range of glaze ingredients may be used, slightly different proportions (e.g. less frit, more clay, feldspar or flint) will be required to achieve the usually higher earthenware maturation range.

6 Widening the colour range

We have already noted that clays differ considerably in colour both before and after firing. Some are white, others pink and sometimes they are speckled. Secondary earthenware clays commonly fire to various shades of orange and dark brown but some fire with a yellow colouration. Most of the colouration in naturally occurring clays is caused by iron which has become mixed with the clay, producing orange to brown shades according to how much iron is present. The more iron there is the darker will be the clay colour. Lime may also be present in the clay and this will produce a yellow colouration. When rust and verdigris (copper 'rust') and Bordeaux mixture containing a copper compound were added to the raku glazes, strong colouration was produced. Similar results can be seen on many medieval English jugs where the thinly applied yellow glazes are speckled with green; where the particles were ground to a very fine powder before mixing with the glaze the colour is much more evenly distributed. Smaller quantities produced weaker colours and larger quantities produced much stronger colours. The powdered bottle glass appeared to lose some intensity of colour when applied as a glaze but was still distinctive. Where iron-bearing clays were mixed in the glazes they too influenced the colours produced. It was also evident that different colours developed in different glazes when the same quantities of iron and copper were used. Sometimes the copper produced green colours, but mixed with a different glaze it produced exciting shades of turquoise. Yet again, if the raku pots were smoke treated (reduced) whilst red hot, the copper-bearing glazes turned brown, blood-red or assumed a metallic copper lustre. With earlier sawdust firings we noticed that sometimes the red clays turned black but patches of pink and red were also evident where more air had reached the pots during firing.

Thus we may conclude so far:

1. Iron often occurs naturally mixed with some clays.
2. Iron and copper can be added to clays and glazes.
3. Iron and copper produce colour in clays and glazes.
4. The more iron or copper used the stronger will be the colour.
5. Coarse iron and copper particles produce speckles of colour.
6. Fine iron and copper particles produce smooth colours.
7. Iron and copper will produce different colours in different glazes.
8. The colours produced by iron and copper are affected by oxidizing and reduction conditions during firing.
9. The basic colour and character of the clay will influence the possible colour range.

Although iron and copper will provide a very satisfying range of colours there are several other very reliable substances which can be used for colouring. They, like copper and iron, are metals. The rust used in earlier experiments is really iron oxide, i.e. iron which has combined with oxygen from the atmosphere. The verdigris is also 'rusted' copper, i.e. copper which has been attacked by carbonic acid (carbon dioxide from the air dissolved in rainwater) to form copper carbonate. Pure metals are seldom used to colour pottery because metal oxides and carbonates are much easier to mix evenly into clays and glazes. The colour of the metal compound (oxide, carbonate etc.) gives no indication of the colours that it will produce when mixed with clays or glazes and fired. Metals such as gold, silver and platinum are used but will not be considered here because they are too expensive. Some metals give very much stronger colouring effects than others so the suggested amounts to be added should be carefully noted.

Some Colouring Compounds

Metal	Compound	Amount	Colour
Chromium	Chromium oxide	1–3%	Usually a heavy green. Yellows and reds in low-temperature lead glazes.
Cobalt	Cobalt oxide Cobalt carbonate	$\frac{1}{2}$–$1\frac{1}{2}$%	Blue.
Copper	Copper oxide Copper carbonate	1–4%	Apple green, turquoise. Red and copper lustre when reduced.
Iron	Black iron oxide Red iron oxide	1–10%	Yellow, red, brown, purple and black when oxidized. Green and blue when reduced.

	Crocus martis Iron spangles		
Manganese	Manganese oxide Manganese carbonate	2–10%	Purple or brown.
Titanium/ Iron	Ilmenite Rutile	1–8%	Textured browns and blues.
Iron/Chrome	Iron chromate	1–3%	Grey.
Nickel	Nickel oxide	1–3%	Soft greys and greens.
Vanadium	Vanadium stain Vanadium pentoxide	5–10%	Yellow (with up to 10% tin oxide).

The colours will alter considerably if different quantities of the compounds are added to different glazes and fired to different temperatures in different atmospheres (oxidized or reduced). Some compounds such as those of copper, melt easily and have a very smooth, fluid appearance in a normally fluid glaze. Others (such as iron chromate) usually look hard and rather dry because they do not melt so easily. Some compounds can be used only at low temperatures because they will 'burn out' (volatilize) at higher temperatures. Quite unexpected and beautiful colours can be obtained by blending different colours but first get to know the individual colour characteristics.

Coloured clays

It is possible to add colour to clay bodies. The effect of iron which occurs naturally in most earthenware clays has already been noted. The amount of iron present in earthenware clays may be as much as ten per cent and in such amounts it plays an important part in lowering the melting point of the clay because it acts as a flux (melting substance). Metallic compounds added to colour clay bodies should therefore be used with caution, especially at higher (stoneware 1300°C) temperatures because they will weaken the body and may cause serious bloating (boiling) in the clay. Also the colours obtained will be rather dull, like dry stones on the beach, and need a glaze over them to 'wet' the colour and develop its richness. Because the clay dulls and absorbs the colour there is a temptation to add more to make the colour stronger. Not only does this weaken the body but it is also a rather expensive way to colour pottery because of the quantities of colouring substance used.

It is difficult to wedge the powdered metal oxide evenly into the plastic clay and, because of the variable moisture content of the clay, the amounts added can only be estimated approximately. For accurate and even colouring the oxide should be mixed in water and sieved into the dried powdered clay after both ingredients have been weighed. Excess water will be required to render the clay sufficiently fluid to stir the ingredients thoroughly together. The coloured clay will then have to be dried to the required working consistency and wedged.

Coloured slips (liquid clay)

Coloured slips are prepared as described above but the clay is used in a much more fluid state—about the consistency of thin cream. The slip should be sieved to remove lumps and distribute the colouring oxides evenly. Smoothest colours are obtained by first carefully grinding the metal oxide, but you may prefer the speckling produced by less finely ground materials. A flour sieve will do but a proper pottery sieve made from phosphor-bronze which will not rust is much better and stronger. If you can afford such a sieve buy a 60-mesh one (i.e. 60 strands to the inch) which will meet most of your needs. The best clays for making slips are the lighter coloured clays which will show the added colours more clearly. Red firing clays can only be used as the basis for dark slips because the amount of iron already present will usually swamp most other colours. It must be remembered that you are adding a thin layer of very wet clay to your damp clay pot and the slip must fit as both it and the pot dry and shrink. Careful judgement is necessary at this point. The clay object must be reasonably damp but firm enough to hold its shape as it absorbs water from the slip and softens. If the clay object is too dry it will probably split as it suddenly swells. Should the clay object be too damp it will soften too much and collapse as it absorbs water from the slip. The slip may appear to fit the clay object at first but it may flake off later if the object is too dry for slipping. Ideally, the moisture from the slip should penetrate the clay body causing the clay particles at the surface to swell and open somewhat, allowing the clay particles of the slip to interlock with the clay particles of the body. As the moisture evaporates, the slip and clay body will bond securely together. If some of the body clay is used in the slip mixture the shrinkage of the slip and the body can be expected to match better.

It is possible to apply slip to biscuit-fired (fired once without glaze) pots, but special adjustments to the slip are necessary to reduce shrinkage since the biscuit-fired pot will have shrunk considerably already. Also, extra fluxes may be required in the slip to make it melt on to the pot in a secure manner. Slip used in this way is approaching the point where it could be considered as a rather dry glaze; the awkward adjustments necessary and the labour involved may make its use hardly worth while when it is considered that it has

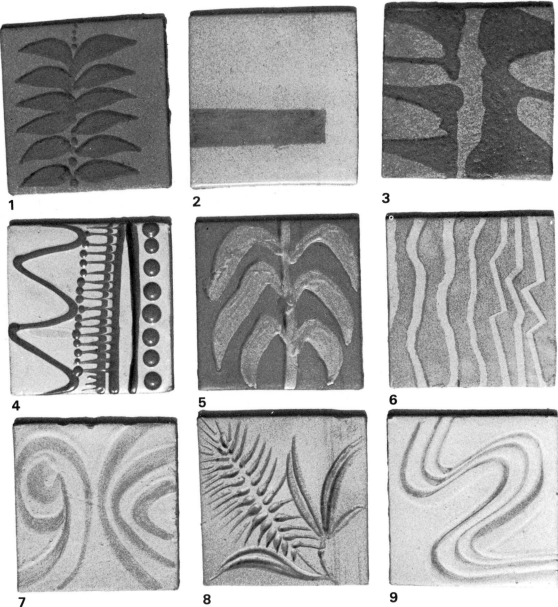

Fig. 59 Slip-decorated tile samples. (1) Brushed-on slip; (2) Panel dipped; (3) Poured; (4) Trailed; (5) Wax resist; (6) Cut paper masking; (7) Brushed-out slip; (8) Slip cut away (scraffito); (9) Wet slip 'combed'

no great advantage over slip applied to a damp, raw body by a simple, direct and reliable process.

Coloured glazes

The same metal compounds which colour slips and bodies may be used to colour glazes. They are mixed in finely powdered form with the glaze. Somewhat smaller quantities can be used since most glazes will usually

79

richen the colours developed, but it is important to note that different glazes fired in different kiln atmospheres (oxidizing or reduced) to different temperatures will often produce strikingly different colours from the same type and quantity of metal oxide.

Directly applied colours

The finely powdered metal oxides can be mixed with water and applied to the object directly at any stage—damp raw, dry raw, biscuited, over slip, before the glaze is applied or after (but usually before the glaze firing). Often glues which burn out during firing are mixed with the metal oxides to make sure they stick on securely and do not smudge with handling. The oxide fluid can be brushed on, sprayed on, stippled on with a sponge, poured on, dabbed on, rubbed in with the hands or applied in any manner that suits the purpose. There is some danger that variations in strength of application will show, e.g. brush lines will show but may be used with advantage. It is more difficult to judge the thickness of application; this can be learned only with experience. The colouring strengths of the metal compounds vary considerably. A thin application of cobalt oxide will give very intense shades of blue. Too much of a strong oxide may merely blacken and blister the glaze or slip. Too little of a weak oxide may disappear entirely. Clean, unfussy and direct application is necessary to avoid disturbing the underlying surface.

Specially prepared body and glaze stains may be bought. These are carefully mixed and refined materials adjusted especially for the particular method of application. They are prepared from the oxides included in the table on pages 76–7 and have attractive names like 'amber orange'. However, they only live up to their names when they are used with the right glaze on a suitable clay body, at the correct temperature and in the right kiln atmosphere, with a suitable firing cycle.

An interesting range of colours may be produced by blending together light and dark firing clays in plastic or slip state. If the clays are kneaded together in the plastic state they will first produce a marbled appearance—a feature exploited in agate ware, popular in medieval English pottery.

Decorating with coloured slips

Usually the coloured slip will contrast with the colour of the clay body to which it is applied, and the contrast may be turned to decorative effect. Basically, the object to be decorated can first be entirely coated with slip which can then be removed in part for decorative effect, or alternatively various means may be used to apply the slip so that areas of the clay body are not coated, again with decorative effect.

Slips can be applied by the following methods:

1. Brushing on.

2. Dipping.
3. Pouring.
4. Trailing, i.e. squeezing the slip in a thin stream from a container with a narrow nozzle—an old plastic detergent container is suitable.

Slips can be withheld from the clay surface by:

1. Waxing.
2. Paper masking.

Slips can be removed for decorative effect by:

1. Brushing off.
2. Scraping off.
3. Combing with a stiff-edged instrument.

These processes may be combined in a wide variety of ways. They are very reliable and enjoyable ways of decorating and are strongly recommended for dependable results throughout the entire range from low-temperature earthenware to high-temperature stoneware.

Slip decoration: techniques

1. *Brushing on.* A fairly fat brush is best because the slip needs to be applied quite thickly. Thin, delicate applications of slip will disappear in firing. The thickness of the slip can be built up by applying several layers but each layer should be allowed to stiffen before the next layer is added if patchy results are to be avoided. The most delicate paint-like qualities of brush decoration can be explored with this technique.

2. *Dipping.* The entire pot may be dipped in the slip to produce a thin, even coating, but it is dangerous to apply slip to both the inside and outside of the pot at the same time because the leather-hard clay will absorb moisture from the slip and there is a risk of collapse if it becomes too wet. Thin-sectioned handles or similar thin projecting parts can be difficult to manage because the moisture of the slip will surround and penetrate the section, thus weakening it. Only careful judgement and experience will determine the right moment for applying slip. Large thin-walled forms with shallow curving bases are also prone to collapse as the weight of the pot bears down on the softened base section. Such difficulties, if anticipated, can be avoided. Perhaps the rim of such a form can be left free of slip and the pot can be stood upside down to dry. Perhaps the slip need only be applied above the danger level of the shallow curved base. Try to anticipate how you will hold and support the pot whilst dipping it. Do not only think about how you will get the pot into the slip but how will you get it out again when it is covered and wet! If a hollow form is turned upside down for dipping air will be trapped inside the form and will prevent the slip entering the pot; the slip container should be of fairly

generous size so that you have freedom of movement. If the pot is partly dipped in the slip, perhaps at an angle, interesting panels will be produced which can often make a pleasant relationship with the form.

3. *Trailing.* Squeezing fluid slip from a pliable bottle with a narrow nozzle (such as a plastic detergent bottle) is a traditional way of applying slip. It is probably best to experiment with this technique on a flat sheet of newspaper before you attempt working on a pot. The consistency of the slip is very important; thin slip will trickle out just at the wrong time but thick slip will produce results rather like icing sugar. Vertical curved surfaces are more difficult to decorate than flat horizontal surfaces. Elaborate patterns can be built up with various sizes of dots which are easier to control than long, thin, straight lines. Keep the bottle well filled with slip and hold the nozzle well below the level of the bottom of the bottle whilst decorating so that the flow of slip is not interrupted by air bubbles. Trailing slip on to a surface which has previously been dipped in slip of contrasting colour produces a very pleasant fluid quality if the background slip is still wet. The nozzle should be held just *above* the surface of the pot. The wet slips may be drawn into delicate shapes by 'feathering', i.e. using a thin flexible point, such as a tip of a feather, to stroke out the slip. Wet slips, gently shaken together, will produce marbled effects but need to be used with extreme caution—control is still essential.

Fig. 60   Trailed-slip decoration being freely applied with a plastic detergent bottle filled with coloured clay of a fluid consistency

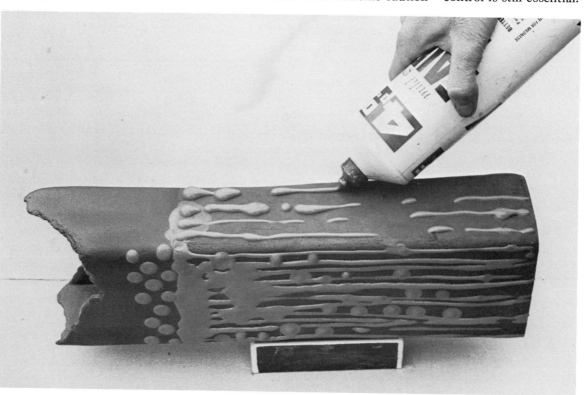

4. *Pouring*. Some shapes are too awkward to dip in slip but they can be stood over a bowl and slip can be poured over them. A form can be entirely coated with slip by this method if appropriate, but sometimes the form will look more interesting before it is entirely covered because the rivulets of slip will flow in interesting paths over it. The direction in which the slip flows may be changed by tilting the form. Also the direction and force with which the slip is poured will have its effect, so intelligent anticipation together with experience will achieve something more than the occasional lucky accident.

Wax-resist painting. Candle wax melted together with machine oil can be painted on to leather-hard clay with a brush. If slip is then poured over this surface it will be repelled by the wax. The slip must not be too thick, however, or it will not flow off the wax. The wax can be melted by placing it in a container stood in a saucepan of boiling water but it must be applied quickly before the wax hardens; the machine oil helps to keep the wax in a fluid state. If the wax is applied with a brush it will have a painted character but there are other ways of applying wax, such as pouring, which will produce different qualities.

Paper masking. Newspaper cut with scissors or freely torn to shape can be tightly stuck to the leather-hard clay by dabbing it into position with a wet

Fig. 61 Applying slip to a cylindrical form by pouring. The decoration is of the paper-resist sort; when the slip has dried to the stage when it has lost its surface shine, the paper may be peeled away leaving the contrasting clay-body colour showing beneath

sponge. Secure contact with the clay surface is essential which makes sharply curved surfaces difficult to deal with by this process. Slip can then be applied by dipping or pouring over the form. When the slip has hardened a little, i.e. when it no longer glistens, the paper shapes may be lifted at the corners and peeled off to show the contrasting background colour beneath. Several layers of slips and paper masking can be built up if desired. This method is very positive and controllable.

Brushed-out decoration. Whilst the freshly applied slip is still glistening wet a fairly stiff brush may be used to brush through the slip. Some slip will thus be removed, revealing the original body colour. The slip will also be forced from beneath the brush, producing a thickening of the slip to the edges of the brush stroke. This can be a very free way of decorating but must be done swiftly and decisively before the slip starts to stiffen.

Combing is very similar to brushing out except that a flexible, stiff-edged tool, such as a strip of plastic cut from a detergent bottle, is used on the wet slip. This sweeps the slip away from its path more sharply and cleanly than the brush.

Fig. 62   The entire plate was first covered with black slip. When the slip was still wet a plastic comb, cut from a detergent bottle, was drawn through it to produce the wavy decoration on the rim. The slip was left to become leather hard and the bird decoration was then cut and scraped away with a pointed knife blade. After biscuit firing, the plate was glazed with a semi-opaque white glaze. Decoration by Bruce, aged 14 years

Scraping ('scraffito'). This process is allied to brushing and combing but is carried out when the slip is leather hard. A pointed knife or loop of wire is used to scrape away the slip cleanly, without producing sharp rough edges on the finished surface. A very broad range of textures can be produced by this method.

This new range of decorative techniques and colours opens a wide area for exploration but it can also introduce new dangers. Colour and decoration must be applied with extreme caution if they are to enhance the form. You must think very carefully about a satisfactory relationship between form, colour and decoration. There are no strict guidelines which can be laid down in this matter; it is very much a question of what feels right. Often the simplest statements are the most effective.

7 Making and firing an electric kiln

The firing procedures outlined so far have progressed from sawdust and open firings to updraught Roman kilns and downdraught raku kilns. Fuels such as sawdust and peat, wood, coke, coal, oil and, perhaps, bottled gas may have been used. The fun, excitement, fascination and challenge of applying fire and flame in a controlled manner to work its effect on clay and glaze will have proved a satisfying and fulfilling experience for those fortunate enough to have access to suitable situations for such activities. But many are denied these opportunities because they live in densely populated urban areas. If you are six floors up in a high-rise block of flats a wood-fired raku kiln is out of the question. The only answer in this situation is an electric kiln.

The particular advantage of an electric kiln is that it operates quietly and it does not burn fuel which produces smoke. There is no firebox or flue and therefore electric kilns are much more compact. An efficient, well designed electric kiln can be more consistent than many flame-fired kilns which can be fairly radically affected by weather conditions, which may slow or speed up the kiln draughts. Electric energy is there at the turn of a switch and the kiln will need attention only periodically during the firing to increase the energy input, whereas kilns using other sources of energy may need almost constant attention. The disadvantage of an electric kiln is that it is not very suitable for reduction firings (i.e. where the kiln atmosphere is deprived of oxygen) because the exposed electric elements will be attacked under such conditions and their life will be shortened according to the degree and duration of the reduction. Reduction atmospheres are often preferred because they produce interesting colour variations in glazes and clay bodies (see chapters 5 and 6). Electric kilns are available in a very wide range of sizes. In industry enormous tunnel kilns are used in which the pottery is loaded on to trolleys which are drawn very slowly through the kiln tunnel. The zone of maximum heat is maintained continuously in the middle region of the tunnel so that the pottery is heated slowly to maximum temperature as it moves through the tunnel and cooled slowly as it moves to the tunnel exit, away from the maximum heat zone. This is a very efficient method since it is a continuous process. The much smaller kilns used by studio potters are packed when cold, heated slowly to maximum temperature and then cooled again for unloading; the whole kiln structure as well as the pots has to be heated and cooled with each firing, which results in some wastage of heat. Efficient insulation of the kiln will save much heat loss although the initial building cost will be greater because good insulating materials are expensive.

The amount of electricity used to heat equally insulated kilns to a given temperature will be in proportion to the size of the kiln. The normal 13-amp domestic power supply will only be sufficient for a very small electric kiln. If you wish to install a larger electric kiln requiring a heavier power input you should first obtain an estimate for the cost of installing the heavier power line which, in most instances, will represent a significant proportion of the capital outlay. The problems of design involving even heat distribution, wiring circuits, switching and control mechanisms become increasingly more involved with larger electric kilns. They are problems best left to experts and are too complex to be considered here. A comprehensive range of commercially produced electric kilns are available at various prices (see list of suppliers). A small electric kiln run off the 13-amp domestic power supply is, however, a fairly simple matter which the enthusiast should be able to tackle with confidence.

Kiln size

The maximum size of kiln which can effectively be run from the 13-amp domestic power supply will be determined by the maximum temperatures required, the quality of the insulating materials used to construct the kiln and the capabilities of the heating elements used. Heat from an electric element is transmitted to the kiln chamber by radiation. The contents of the kiln take up this heat and it is further distributed by conduction and radiation through the kiln load. The distances across which the heat will travel are determined by the heat energy produced by the kiln elements and the heat-conducting capabilities of the kiln contents. For support purposes the elements are set in grooves in the kiln walls and the heat has to be capable of spreading fairly evenly from the elements to the centre of the kiln. There is a limit to the amount of energy provided by the 13-amp supply and consequently in the heat produced by an electric element. The amount of heat produced by the element will be capable of heating a small space to a higher temperature than a larger space. Thus if we wish to fire only to earthenware temperatures (1100°C) we can build a larger kiln chamber than if we wish to fire to stoneware temperatures (1300°C). The recommended kiln sizes are

$9 \times 9 \times 9$ inches (internally) for stoneware and $12 \times 12 \times 12$ inches (internally) for earthenware. Beyond these limits there will be a progressive deterioration of performance which will be reflected in uneven heating and shortening of the element's life.

The kiln structure

The materials used in the kiln structure should be chosen for their insulating properties. Good insulating materials are usually rather expensive but will repay their initial cost in terms of electricity saved. Inferior insulating materials contain substances which will not withstand the intense heat produced in the immediate vicinity of the elements. If good insulating materials are used the thickness of the kiln wall will need to be only about $4\frac{1}{2}$ inches. Either insulating bricks or a castable insulating cement can be used. Insulating bricks can easily be cut with an old saw blade; they can also be drilled and there is no need to cement the bricks because they are machined with accurate square faces and can be assembled dry. If a castable cement is used it will be necessary to make casting moulds, but the element grooves can be cast into the slabs in one operation. The inside face of the slab must be cast in alumina-rich, iron-free cement to a depth of at least $2\frac{1}{2}$ inches but this can be backed with a cheaper insulating material such as vermiculite and Ciment Fondu. Note the manufacturer's instructions carefully. Do not mix the cement with too much water. The bricks or slabs will require a light-weight angle-iron framework to hold them in position, e.g. Dexian.

The elements

The filament of an electric torch bulb is similar in many respects to an electric kiln element. When the electric circuit is completed by switching on the torch the tungsten bulb filament immediately heats and the bright glow is used as a light source. A low-voltage bulb has a thinner filament than a higher voltage bulb. The voltage produced by the torch batteries must be matched with the bulb; if the battery voltage is too low for the bulb the filament will not heat up enough, indeed it may not even glow. If the battery voltage is too high for the bulb the filament may glow brightly for a moment and then 'burn out' or melt with the heat. The wire element of an electric fire is very much thicker and longer and requires a much higher voltage to make it glow red hot and give off heat. The thickness of the wire element and its length are very carefully calculated to match the voltage which will be passed through it. The electric-kiln element is, again, much thicker and if it is made of a special metal called kanthal (grade A1) it will withstand heating to a very high temperature (1300°C); it can be obtained from the suppliers, ready wound in various lengths and thicknesses calculated to match the voltages with which it will be used. The normal domestic voltage is usually 240 V. The voltage may be loosely described as the amount of 'push' behind the electric current.

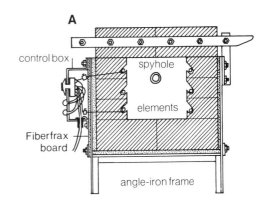

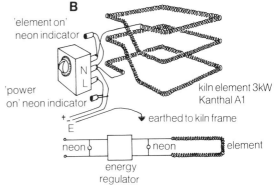

Fig. 64 (A) Diagram of the construction of an electric kiln; (B) Diagram showing wiring detail

Fig. 63 The basic structure of a small electric kiln capable of stoneware temperatures and run from a normal 13-amp domestic power supply. The framework is Dexian-type and the dry-brick construction of high grade insulation blocks (List of components and suppliers appears on page 136)

The *power* that is radiated into the kiln in the form of heat is measured in *watts* and this is determined by the *resistance* of the element. A two-bar electric fire uses 2000 watts or 2 kilowatts per hour. The electric energy is converted to heat energy. The electric kiln will need a 3-kilowatt element (or three 1-kilowatt elements). The heat from this element will be trapped within the insulated kiln and after a period of time will heat the kiln contents to the required temperature. This type of kiln is capable of firing to the highest temperatures necessary for most pottery (except high-temperature porcelain 1300°C +). Although it is possible to reach temperatures of up to 1300°C it is advisable to fire somewhat below this temperature (1280°C maximum) if the life of the element is to be prolonged. Once the element has been fired it will become rather brittle and will break easily if handled carelessly. If it becomes essential to move the element after firing for any reason this will be more safely achieved if it is gently heated by switching the kiln on—but don't forget to switch off again before touching the element.

The controls

It would be quite possible to connect the ends of the heating element, one to the live and the other to the neutral feeds from the 13-amp supply, switch on and wait until the desired temperature is reached, but you would have no control over the speed of heating within the kiln. Such control can be achieved by two different methods:

1. You could have three separate 1-kilowatt elements to provide the required heat. The first element could be switched on for low heat, the second for medium heat and the third for maximum heat. The small commercially produced kilns with low, medium, high switches may employ this method. Alternatively, two 1·5-kilowatt elements can be used, coupled in series for low temperature; using only one element (probably the lower one since the heat will rise and therefore be more evenly distributed) for medium temperature; and coupled in parallel for maximum temperature. The placing and spacing of the elements will have to be so arranged that heating is as even as possible throughout the kiln at all times.

2. A much simpler and preferable method is to use a single 3-kilowatt element with an energy regulator in the circuit. An electric oven simmerstat which can be obtained quite cheaply from any large electric suppliers will be suitable. You might even obtain a working simmerstat from a scrapped oven. According to the setting of the simmerstat the electric current is switched on and off for longer or shorter periods. Naturally, the longer the on-period the hotter the element will become. Very gradual and finely controlled temperature rises are possible by this means. The element's life will probably be prolonged too since the heat from the element is being conducted away from the element whether it is on or off; only in the latter stages of firing will it build up an area of extreme heat in its immediate vicinity. You will probably be able to hear a gentle hum whilst the current is flowing through the electric element but a neon pilot-light wired across the leads feeding the element will be a clearer and safer indication that electricity is flowing through the element. Another pilot-light wired across the power feed before the simmerstat will show when the supply is switched on. A cut-out switch on the power feed line which is operated when the lid is raised and lowered is a highly recommended safety feature but the switch must be suitably rated for this job.

The couplings to the element should be securely made with porcelain or brass connectors to asbestos-coated copper wire. Plastic or rubber-sleeved power cable should be used only where it cannot be melted by the heat of the kiln. The leads and element ends should be routed well away from the angle-iron framework and thoroughly insulated. Unnecessarily long element tails and power leads are a danger and source of heat loss. Keep the element tails as short as possible. Fold and twist the tail back on itself two or three times before tightening it into the connector; this will effectively reduce the resistance and diminish the amount of heat dissipated along the leads. Make sure that the kiln is well earthed on the frame. The control box housing the simmerstat and pilot-lights is usually fixed to the kiln framework but it must be insulated from the heat of the kiln. There is no particular reason why it cannot be situated independently away from the kiln; it should not be possible to twist, bend or pull the power cable as this will fracture the wires and break down the insulation.

Calibrating the simmerstat

As already stated, the simmerstat will switch on and off automatically for variable periods according to the setting. Make a mark or notch on the control knob opposite another mark on the mount when the switch is in the off position. Now advance the knob, switching on the current. Make another mark on the mount opposite the new position of the mark on the knob. Use a watch with a sweep second hand to count how long the current remains switched on in this position. If, for example, the current is on for twelve seconds and off for thirty-six seconds this represents an on-phase of one third which can be marked on the mount accordingly. Then make trials and calibrations in a range of different positions until you reach the continuously-on position; the scale will tend to become much closer as you approach this position. This will give no indication of the actual temperature within the kiln but it will show the proportion of time during which heat is being generated and thus an indication of the relative rate of temperature increase.

The spy-hole

A reasonably large spy-hole ($1\frac{1}{4}$ inches tapering to 1 inch) with a well-fitting bung should be cut through the brick or cast in the slab so that the interior of the kiln can be viewed from time to time, but never poke into this hole anything which might touch an element when the kiln is on. The top of the kiln chamber may be hotter than the floor of the chamber (since heat rises) so the spyhole should be situated midway up for the region of average heat. In larger kilns more than one spy-hole is necessary. Make sure that the spy-hole entry is well clear of the elements.

Telling the temperature

With experience it is possible to estimate the kiln temperature by colour (see guide chart on page 131) but there is no evident colour until the kiln has reached about 500°C. The only accurate way to measure temperature at all stages of firing is by means of a thermocouple and pyrometer but this apparatus is expensive; it will cost as much as the small kiln itself and, furthermore, it only reliably indicates the rise or fall of temperature within the kiln.

The apparatus does not indicate what effect the temperature is having on the pots and glazes because this is very much a question of temperature *and* the length of time during which the pots are exposed to the heat. The work being done by the heat is best determined by pyrometric cones. These cones are composed of certain materials which melt at predetermined temperatures. It is usual to place two or three cones in the kiln where they can be seen through the spy-hole. One cone is selected which will melt at the maximum time/temperature stage desired, showing that the heat has done the required work. The other two cones can be selected to melt at lower temperatures as a warning that maximum temperature will soon be reached. These cones are cheap, reliable and virtually indispensable. They are available for all necessary firing temperatures between 800°C and 1300°C and beyond.

Packing the kiln

Kiln furniture, obtainable from listed suppliers, is necessary to enable full use of the kiln space. The furniture is made from material which can withstand frequent heating to high temperatures. It comes in all shapes and sizes but for this electric kiln you will need only shelves $7\frac{1}{2} \times 7\frac{1}{2} \times \frac{3}{8}$ inches and interlocking props, about a dozen each of $1\frac{1}{2}$ inches and 1 inch, high-temperature quality. If you have any spare pieces of insulating brick these can easily be ground into shapes suitable for shelf supports for this small kiln. In larger kilns, where loadings are much heavier, such supports would not survive the compressive forces, but pieces of stronger firebrick could be used instead. The shelves and the kiln contents should not be placed too close to

Fig. 65 Kiln packing showing arrangement of shelves and props

92

the sides of the kiln otherwise the heat will not circulate and hot spots will develop which will overheat the pots and damage the elements. Usually it is unnecessary to use kiln furniture for biscuit firing since the raw pots may be stood in and on each other provided they are free to contract and provided their weight is evenly distributed and supported, but glazed pottery must be packed as closely as possible without actually touching. The glaze should be wiped back at least $\frac{1}{4}$ of an inch from any part of an object which is in contact with any part of the kiln floor or shelving. More fluid and thickly or unevenly applied glazes may run down and stick the object to the kiln shelf, seriously damaging both shelf and pot. For this reason the shelf should be brushed over with a mixture of two parts flint to three parts china clay mixed with water.

Firing the kiln

Biscuit firing should be started very slowly so that moisture in the clay can escape slowly, as mentioned previously (at least one hour for the first 100°C). A rise of 100°C per hour is slow enough for both biscuit and glaze firings. This small kiln can be fired very much more quickly but the temptation to hurry the firings should be resisted; a stoneware glaze firing to 1280°C should not take less than eight hours. (See ideal firing graphs on page 113 for further information.) The 800–900°C phase of biscuit firing should also be taken slowly (one and a half to two hours) with the spy-hole bung removed to give maximum ventilation so that any carbon in the body can be burned out. If the kiln is formed from cast slabs it should be fired empty to about 900°C for the first firing. This firing should be *very* slow to 'cure' the cast slabs if cracking is to be avoided. Your patience will be well rewarded. The first firing of the dry-jointed insulating-brick kiln can be taken at normal speed since the bricks are free to expand and contract without cracking. Make sure that the bricks are pushed tightly together. Leave the nuts securing the lid tie-bars slightly loose for careful tightening when the kiln is orange hot. Clays containing carbon and sulphurous minerals may smell slightly during the firing. Dust on new bricks and elements will also smell a little as they are burned in the early stages of firing a new kiln but there is no cause for alarm.

If these notes and the associated diagrams are followed carefully it is an easy matter to build and fire your own small electric kiln which will enable you to produce a fairly comprehensive range of wares, limited only in size. The wiring circuits are elementary and this electric kiln, if used sensibly, is less dangerous than an electric fire.

8 The stoneware range

Materials

In basic principle there is no great difference between the raku kiln and a kiln which will fire to stoneware temperatures (1250–1300°C). The building materials, however, will have to withstand the higher temperatures; ordinary housing bricks will melt if used for the inner kiln walls. Good-quality firebricks must be used in the firebox and other areas subjected to direct flame because they are very refractory, i.e. they can withstand very high temperatures, but they do not have good insulating properties and will not hold the heat in very well. The expense of an outer layer of good-quality insulating bricks or concrete will be repaid by the fuel, time and money saved in bringing the kiln to the required temperature. The entire kiln could be made from castable cements provided a refractory mix, backed by an insulating mix to hold in the heat, is used for those parts which will be subjected to the greatest heat. Ciment Fondu is an alumina-rich cement suitable for casting kiln sections but its insulating or fractory properties are dependent upon the aggregates with which it is mixed. The higher the alumina content of the brick aggregate the greater will be the refractoriness of the concrete:

> Crushed red-brick aggregate—up to 1000°C.
> Crushed firebrick 25% alumina—up to 1300°C.
> Crushed firebrick 40% alumina—up to 1400°C.
> Sillimanite is used for even greater refractoriness.

Some parts of the kiln (e.g. the firebox) may be considerably hotter than the inside of the kiln chamber.

The size of the aggregate is determined by the thickness of the concrete section. Careful grading of the aggregate, from the maximum size downwards, is also essential to the strength of the mix. Too much fine material produces a weak mix and greater shrinkage whereas a harsh mix, which is difficult to compact and from which the water will readily bleed, results if too little fine aggregate is used.

Casting thickness	Aggregate	Fondu
Up to 2 in.	$\frac{1}{8}$ in.–dust: $2\frac{1}{2}$ volumes	1 volume
2–6 in.	$\frac{3}{8}$–$\frac{1}{8}$ in.: 2 volumes $\frac{1}{8}$ in.–dust: 2 volumes	1 volume
Above 6 in.	$\frac{3}{4}$–$\frac{1}{8}$ in.: 3 volumes $\frac{1}{8}$ in.–dust: 2 volumes	1 volume

Used at stoneware temperatures some of the Fondu will act as a flux and produce a ceramic bond in the concrete. Too much cement in the mixture will over flux the concrete; too little will produce a weak concrete below 900°C before the fluxing action starts.

The aggregate should be soaked before use to encourage good mixing, but excess water will weaken the concrete. After soaking and draining the aggregate little further water will be required when the cement is added. A suitable insulating mix would be 4 volumes of vermiculite to 1 volume of Fondu cement. Approximately $1\frac{1}{4}$ gallons of water will be required for every 10 pounds of cement and approximately $5\frac{1}{2}$ hundredweights of cement will be needed for 1 cubic yard of concrete. Very smooth mould faces will produce harder and more dense faces to the cast form. Wooden moulds faced with polythene sheets are excellent if the concrete is well settled but excessive puddling will weaken the surface by drawing out the water. Allow twenty-four hours for the concrete to cure and cover with damp sacking during this time to prevent rapid moisture evaporation which will weaken the concrete.

Basic design
It is important to remember that much heat can be lost downwards through the kiln floor; a good insulating pad on which to build the kiln will save more heat. Efficient use of heat within the kiln is extremely important if high temperatures are required so flame routing must be carefully considered. At first, space should be provided for the flame to develop; an early and sudden change of direction in the flame path should be avoided especially if the fuel is pressurized (gas or oil). The most natural direction for the flame to travel is upwards because hot air rises. If the flame is introduced in a horizontal direction low down in the kiln its natural tendency will cause it to turn upwards and rise to the top 'crown' of the kiln. If the entrance to the flue is situated in the top of the kiln the heat will pass directly out (as in the Roman kiln); this is

known as an 'up-draught' kiln system which is not a very efficient way to use heat. If, however, the flue entrance is situated at or below the floor level of the kiln chamber, the flame will rise as before to the top of the kiln and then have to come down to escape through the flue at floor level. This is called a 'down-draught' system or, more plainly, an up-and-down-draught system. As the flue is warmed, the speed at which the waste gases rise up the chimney increases and a heat-flow path is established. To raise the temperature the fuel rate is slowly increased; at the same time more air is drawn into the kiln to provide oxygen for burning the fuel and the heat flow speeds up. Variable controls (dampers) are necessary at the flue to alter the apertures and hence the speed at which the gases pass through the kiln.[1] Air mixed with the fuel at the firebox entry is called primary air but additional secondary air is often drawn into the flame path to allow more complete burning of the fuel.

The area in which the pots will be stood for firing should not be directly in the flame path otherwise uneven heating will probably occur. A protective 'bag-wall' may be necessary to protect the pots and to coax the flame along its correct path. At one time pots were often stood in clay boxes (saggers) to protect them from direct flame but this precaution is not essential with the fuels and kiln designs in use today.

The size of the kiln is also important. Unless you anticipate production in quantity there can be a frustrating time-lag whilst you amass enough pots to fill a large kiln, whereas a small kiln fired more frequently will provide invaluable experience. Small kilns below 20 cubic feet are, however, more expensive to operate and more difficult to manage efficiently.

Fuels

Wood, oil and propane gas are very suitable for stoneware firings but will have to be considered with a view to availability, cost and convenience. Wood and oil may have to be excluded if you are in a smokeless zone although a well conducted firing should not produce volumes of smoke. The ash which is carried into the kiln from a wood fire affects the stoneware pots and glazes in an often advantageous manner, but wood is not always readily available in sufficient quantity and stoking is a time-consuming process. Oil is a convenient fuel and, despite escalating costs, it is still not a prohibitively costly one.

Oil burners

There are two different types of oil burner:

1.   Natural draught burners (drip feed). (See Fig. 70.) These are placed at

---

[1] For kiln properties and construction see:
Bernard Leach *A Potter's Book* (Faber & Faber, London), pp. 190–193.
Daniel Rhodes *Kilns: Design, Construction and Operation* (A & C Black, London).

Fig. 66 *Small stoneware kiln which could be fired with wood, propane gas or oil. The firebox is at the rear of the kiln and is a loose brick construction which can be adjusted to suit the fuel in use*

Fig. 67 *Diagram of the stoneware kiln shown in fig. 66. This small kiln is very efficient; it employs a down-draught-plus system. The heat rises naturally to the top of the kiln chamber but has to descend again to escape through the several ports situated at kiln chamber floor level—up to this point the down-draught system operates. However, before the exhaust gases are able to escape up the chimney they are circulated round the outside walls of the kiln chamber, thus taking maximum advantage of the heat delivered*

spyhole

door

kiln chamber

firebox

fire bars

ash pit

the firebox entrance and consist of a stepped series of sloped, louvered iron plates on to which the oil is dripped. Initially, an oil-soaked cloth or porous brick is lit beneath the plates to heat them and start the burning process; as the plates become heated so the oil will burn as it drips on to them. Air is drawn into the fire through the louvers. In the early stages bricks are stood partly in front of the burner plates to prevent an excessive intake of air which would only chill the plates. As the fire is established and the firebox warms, the oil flow is gradually increased and then water is dripped in with the oil. The beads of water immediately form steam and assist in 'cracking' the oil, thus speeding combustion. Too much water will chill the plates and slow combustion; and careful observation of the flame will indicate whether more or less oil, air or water is needed. Pre-heated secondary air, drawn under the firebox and delivered to the oil flame, will greatly improve combustion. A reservoir tank for oil and one for water will need to be placed at sufficient height to provide a steady gravity-induced flow which can be delivered by

Fig. 68 Catenary arch construction of the oil-fired stoneware kiln

polythene tubing clipped to an angle-iron channel. Simple screw clips on the tubing will suffice to regulate the oil and water flows. If some arrangement can be made to spread the oil/water delivery across the plates so much the better as this will increase the burning-surface area.

2. Forced air burners. Forced air is used to disintegrate the oil into a fine spray. The minute droplets of oil present a vastly increased surface area and combustion is swift and complete. Cheap, second-hand vacuum cleaners are very suitable as a source of forced air and burners can be made up from readily available plumbing fitments, as shown in the diagrams on page 101. It is advisable to treat the power supply to the vacuum cleaners with care since they will require 240/250 V which can be lethal if inadequately earthed and weatherproofed in wet conditions. Weatherproof connections and overhead leads are essential. A gravity-induced oil feed delivered through polythene tubing and regulated with a screw clamp at the burner is adequate. The reservoir will need to be placed at sufficient height (6–8 feet) to supply a steady flow of oil at maximum consumption rate. A kiln of 20 cubic feet will need 3–4 gallons of oil per hour and total consumption should be approximately 30 gallons.

98

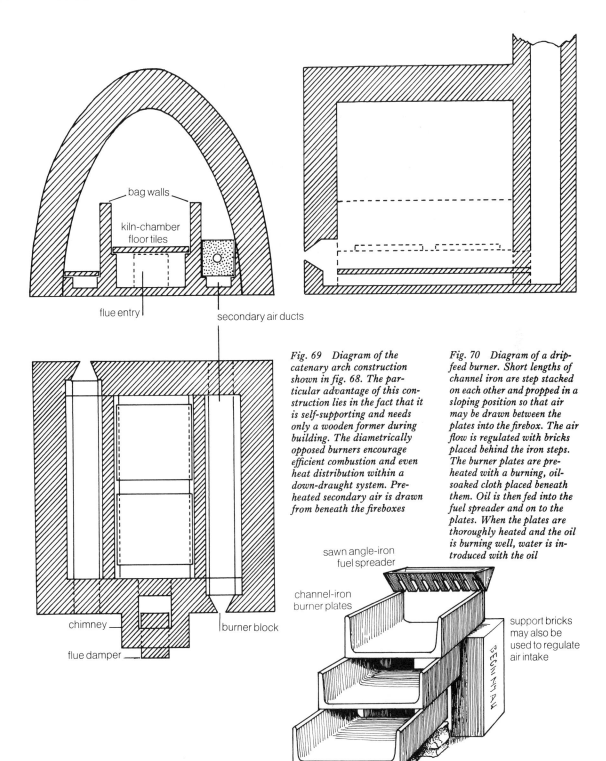

bag walls

kiln-chamber
floor tiles

flue entry

secondary air ducts

chimney

flue damper

burner block

sawn angle-iron
fuel spreader

channel-iron
burner plates

support bricks
may also be
used to regulate
air intake

Fig. 69 *Diagram of the catenary arch construction shown in fig. 68. The particular advantage of this construction lies in the fact that it is self-supporting and needs only a wooden former during building. The diametrically opposed burners encourage efficient combustion and even heat distribution within a down-draught system. Preheated secondary air is drawn from beneath the fireboxes*

Fig. 70 *Diagram of a dripfeed burner. Short lengths of channel iron are step stacked on each other and propped in a sloping position so that air may be drawn between the plates into the firebox. The air flow is regulated with bricks placed behind the iron steps. The burner plates are preheated with a burning, oil-soaked cloth placed beneath them. Oil is then fed into the fuel spreader and on to the plates. When the plates are thoroughly heated and the oil is burning well, water is introduced with the oil*

99

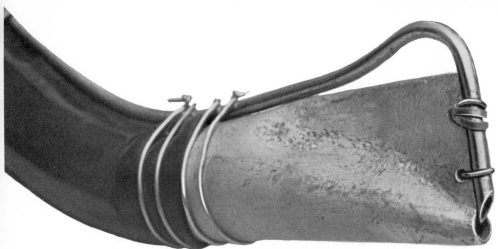

Fig. 71 Vacuum-tube burner, forced draught

Fig. 72 A vacuum cleaner producing forced air for an oil burner made from standard plumbing fitments. The oil is supplied through a gravity-induced feed and regulated by the screw clamp

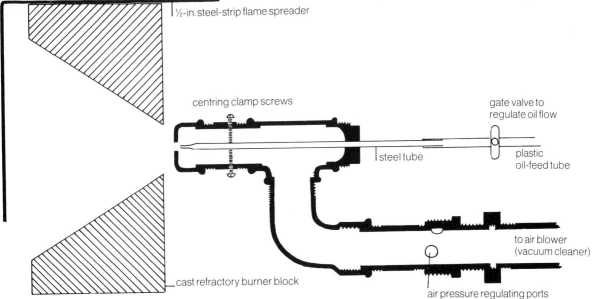

½-in. steel-strip flame spreader

centring clamp screws

gate valve to regulate oil flow

steel tube

plastic oil-feed tube

to air blower (vacuum cleaner)

cast refractory burner block

air pressure regulating ports

Fig. 73 Diagram of the forced-air oil burner made from standard plumbing fitments: cap; T-junction (a 'swept' T-junction is preferable); plug; elbow; short connecting sections; an 18 × ½ × ⅛ inch steel tube; gate clamp; 1 foot × ¼ inch steel tube; a suitable length of ¼-inch plastic tubing; vacuum cleaner with flexible tube. The strength of the forced-air draught is regulated by a threaded 'sleeve' which is used to open or close the two ports in the tube from the air blower. The flow of oil is regulated by a gate valve. For a small flame less oil and air are required, but the 'flame spreader' strip produces better turbulence and mixing of the oil and air. The oil tube is flattened at the end to produce a more effective jet and the aperture in the cap is correspondingly oval in shape (5/16 × 13/16 inch). The oil jet is secured by centring clamp screws which enable the jet to be moved forwards or backwards, thus effecting the shape and length of the flame. The conical shape of the burner block encourages the development of a well-shaped flame. At high temperatures the spreader strip may be removed. Reduction atmospheres are produced by reducing primary and/or secondary air intake

Waste sump oil can be burned with the drip-feed burner but it is advisable to strain the oil first to remove sludge lumps which may clog the flow. Thirty-five-second gas oil or paraffin oil is necessary for the forced-air burners although some sump oil could be mixed with this for economy.

Propane burners

Propane burners cannot be made very easily and are best purchased from reputable suppliers who can advise on the type of burner required, jet sizes etc., all of which will need to be calculated according to kiln size and maximum consumption rates. If gas is drawn from a propane cylinder at a fast rate, the cylinder will soon ice up. This will result in a drop in gas pressure which can only be overcome by switching to a fresh cylinder. A large kiln requiring a heavy off-take will need several cylinders connected by special switching valves and this adds to the cost and complicates the system. However, a simple torch burner and a 56-pound cylinder can be combined to make an efficient, portable and clean set-up for use with a small kiln of 1½–2 cubic feet.

Stoneware clays

Stoneware firings (1250–1300°C) require a different range of clays and glazes. Most local clays used in previously described processes will be too fusable (meltable) at these temperatures. Ball clays, china clays and fire clays form the basis of most stoneware materials but they have a limited distribution and specially prepared stoneware clays will probably need to be purchased from reputable suppliers (see page 115).

101

Stoneware glazes

The additional cost of prepared clays is, however, largely offset by the considerable saving on stoneware glaze materials. At stoneware temperatures there are often locally available rocks and minerals that will produce interesting melts, but to identify their potential it is preferable to prepare them in a finely ground state when they will become more chemically reactive. Clay is ideal in this respect because it is so easily ground to a fine powder but other rocks may require more time and energy in preparation. Some rocks will grind better if they have been heated previously since this will 'loosen' their structure; flints, for example, will respond well to this treatment but they may also shatter violently and should be covered carefully to prevent the hazard of flying pieces. Some rocks are already available in finely powdered form as scouring powders. Calcined bones (or bonemeal) provides an interesting material, as do many other garden fertilizers. Pieces of cake-soap and flaked soap will produce surprising results because they contain soda and potash which will form a glaze with clay, and vegetable and wood ashes have

Fig. 74   Local rocks tested at stoneware temperatures

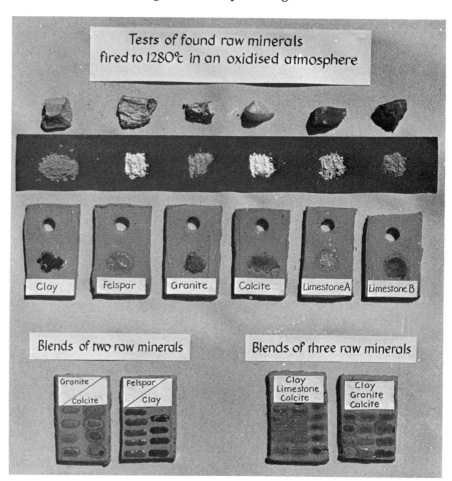

102

provided the essential ingredients for many beautiful glazes. It is both rewarding and informative to make a collection of finely-ground materials and to fire them separately on a flat sheet of stoneware clay marked off in 1¼-inch squares, with each substance clearly identified. If the samples are duplicated they can be fired at earthenware (1050–1100°C) and stoneware (1250–1300°C) temperatures which will produce some further interesting comparisons. Mix each material with a little water to a thin paste and deposit it in a small blob.

A sample test tile could be prepared as follows:

Soap	Powdered local clay	Scouring powder	Baking powder
Table salt	Garden fertilizer	Wood ash	Washing soda
Bonemeal	Crushed granite chips	Chalk	Crushed slate

Although it might be possible to arrive at satisfactory glazes from suitable mixtures of these and similar materials, a short list of prepared minerals will prove very useful, more consistent and labour-saving for glaze preparation in quantity. The following are recommended and should be similarly tested so that you become conversant with their basic characteristics.

China clay	Potash feldspar	Dolomite	Borax frit
Ball clay	Cornish stone	Magnesium carbonate	Lead monosilicate frit
Flint	Whiting	Barium carbonate	Alkaline frit

The tests fired to earthenware temperature will show less dramatic changes (except for the frits) than the stoneware-temperature tests. After firing the stoneware tests it will be noted that some materials have:

1. Melted completely into a glassy patch—*fluxed*, e.g. frits, ash, soap.
2. Fused into a hard shiny lump and stuck securely to the tile—*fluxed but remained viscous*, e.g. potash feldspar, cornish stone, granite, scouring powder, local clay.
3. Hardened without obvious signs of melting—*remained refractory*, e.g. flint, china clay, ball clay, bonemeal.

103

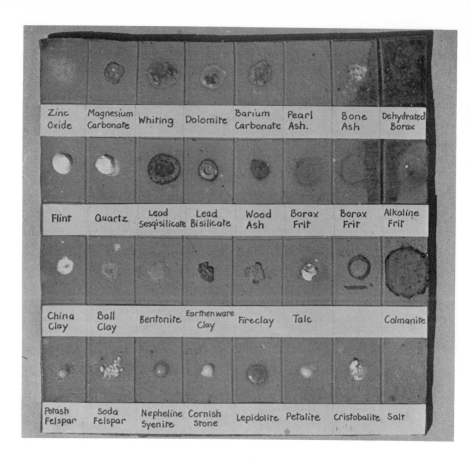

Zinc Oxide	Magnesium Carbonate	Whiting	Dolomite	Barium Carbonate	Pearl Ash.		Bone Ash	Dehydrated Borax
Flint	Quartz	Lead Sesqisilicate	Lead Bisilicate	Wood Ash	Borax Frit		Borax Frit	Alkaline Frit
China Clay	Ball Clay	Bentonite	Earthenware Clay	Fireclay	Talc			Colmanite
Potash Felspar	Soda Felspar	Nepheline Syenite	Cornish Stone	Lepidolite	Petalite		Cristobalite	Salt

Fig. 75   Mineral test tile

Comparing the earthenware and stoneware tiles it will be obvious that the amount of fusion and melting is associated with temperature. The higher the temperature the better the melt.

Acute observation of results is recommended because some reactions may belie the potential of the material. Whiting, for example, does not appear to melt very much until the edges of the sample are examined. Where clay and whiting have made contact there is a much stronger reaction and the melting eats into the clay, i.e. the material is *corrosive*. The same is true of barium carbonate and dolomite. Some materials show small or large 'halos' round them—especially salt and the frits. This is an indication that they are becoming *volatile*. Some materials will perform in a manner which makes it difficult to define them clearly within these terms because often they are compounds (natural or manufactured) of several different materials and even these compounds are not necessarily stable. Cornish stone, for example, may vary from one source of supply to another—which explains why someone else's glaze recipe may not work for you if your source of supply is different.

104

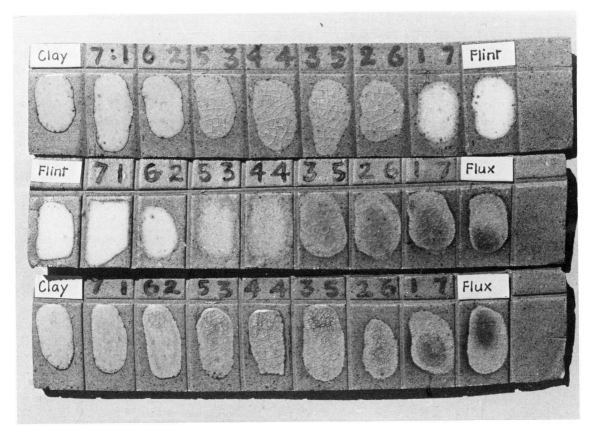

Glaze ingredients

There are various materials (fluxes) which play an active part in melting a glaze, but glaze viscosity is largely controlled by the proportion of *alumina* present and its hardness (refractoriness) by the proportion of *silica* present. This statement is necessarily a very sweeping generalization, made in an attempt to avoid getting too deeply involved in the chemistry of glazing whilst providing a very simplified explanation of the material tests outlined previously. In simplified examples the composition of these materials is now represented, for purposes of comparison, in terms of these three ingredients, i.e. fluxes (F), alumina (A), silica (S). (See glaze ingredient analysis graphs, p. 133)

These three ingredients are essential to a glaze but their relative proportions in a workable glaze will vary with the temperature at which the glaze is required to melt and the characteristic qualities of the glaze. Low-temperature glazes are proportionately higher in fluxes and vice versa. Silica is the essential basis of glass but the fluxes are required in the correct proportion to make it melt within the required range, and alumina gives the viscosity necessary to stop the glaze flowing off the pots.

Comparing the sample histograms and the fired test tiles, a clearer un-

105

derstanding should now emerge. On the stoneware-fired tile it will be seen that feldspar and Cornish stone could be used as glazes almost without further adjustment. The histograms show why—they contain all three essential ingredients. Just a little more flux is all that is required, i.e. some more of one of the better melted samples. Flint, on the other hand, contains no flux or alumina and whiting contains no alumina or silica so neither of these materials alone can produce a glaze. Moreover, within this range of ingredients we have some which are strongly predominant in fluxes, e.g. whiting, ash, magnesium carbonate and dolomite. For these flint will provide silica but there is no predominate source of alumina which can be used to balance the glaze. Fortunately the clays—china clay and ball clay—are fairly rich in alumina and if we look again at the feldspar and Cornish stone histograms we will see that the proportion of alumina present is not very high (15–18 per cent) yet satisfactory stoneware glazes are being approached. Thus we may assume that the proportion of alumina required may not be very high and that it should be possible to provide sufficient from clay sources; but at the same time the silica added (in the clay) will harden the glaze and so to resolve *this* problem more flux (perhaps whiting, dolomite or magnesium carbonate) will be needed to balance out the additional silica. A correct balance is what is required and the understanding necessary to enable you to tip the balance in the direction in which you wish to move.

Initially, start with mixtures of two (or at most three) materials so that results are easily interpreted. Modifications should be made to only one material at a time if confusion is to be avoided. The sample tests and histograms will indicate where your most helpful blends are likely to occur. A blending procedure such as that outlined in chapter 5 will suffice and experience will soon enable you to recognize the more profitable ranges within which to work.

There is an interesting comparison to be drawn between clays and glazes. Just as glazes contain fluxes, alumina and silica, so also do clays, but the refractory clays—china clay, ball clay and fireclay—are high in alumina and silica and very low in fluxes. These clays could be described as glazes with too much alumina and silica; conversely, glazes could be described as clays with excessive amounts of flux. Indeed, the Gault clay, as already mentioned, will function as a glaze at stoneware temperatures because of its high lime content.

Vegetable-ash glazes
Vegetable ashes make interesting glaze ingredients but they must first be carefully prepared. There is a considerable diversity of opinion about preparation but initially the ash must be collected in as clean a condition as possible—no soil or metal pieces! Some potters simply dry-sieve the ash and use it directly; others wash the ash once or several times with water. The feel of the water indicates that something is being washed out of the ash. This

something is soluble alkali which has a fluxing effect within a glaze but, because it is a soluble ingredient, presents problems (see chapter 5). Careful tests indicate that two or three washings are adequate; it is the grade of sieve used in preparation that is much more important. A very fine sieve removes quite large amounts of coarser material from the ash (probably silica) and in consequence the glaze is noticeably more fluxed. Since ashes differ so much it is perhaps unwise to make any rules about preparation; even the same vegetable ash changes very noticeably in some instances in accordance with the seasons! But two washings and sieving through an 80-mesh sieve should be enough. Allow the ash to settle, syphon off as much water as possible and then dry the ash ready for use.

Note: the soluble alkali in ash water is sometimes very caustic and will irritate the skin, so either use rubber gloves during preparation or keep your hands out of the water.

There are some excellent books available which are devoted entirely to the complex subject of glazes and will make interesting reading when a basic understanding has been achieved through experience. Obviously the few paragraphs above can only sketch the briefest outline in very generalized terms, but sensible experimentation and careful observation of results within this suggested framework should produce some very acceptable glazes and a sympathetic feeling for the basic characteristics of some glaze ingredients.

Salt glazing

The reaction of ordinary household salt on the test tile indicated a substance which became volatile (evaporated) at stoneware temperatures. Salt is also corrosive of the clay, boils violently and is soluble. This would not at first suggest a suitable material for use in glazing, but in fact salt is a well proven glazing material. Because it is soluble and volatile it cannot be applied by the usual glazing procedures; instead, its volatile properties are turned to advantage. Raw or biscuit-fired pots, glazed with conventional glazes only where not exposed to the kiln atmosphere, are packed into the kiln as for a normal glaze firing. The pots and lids, etc. are stood securely on small pellets of a china clay/alumina mixture (3 parts alumina to 1 part china clay) to prevent them sticking to the shelves (which are also dressed with a wash consisting of 5 parts alumina hydrate to 1 part china clay) during the firing. The kiln is then fired to stoneware glaze temperature (1260°C). Various patterns of oxidation and reduction may be attempted within the temperature range 1000–1260°C. This, of course, will affect the colour of the body but it is advisable to have a final period of oxidizing before salt glazing is started if a warmer colour range is preferred. Dampers and burners are then controlled to give a light reduction atmosphere and damp salt wrapped in paper is thrown into the firebox. The intense heat causes the salt to vaporize and the kiln chamber is rapidly filled with hydrogen chloride gas and soda vapour.

The soda vapour has a natural affinity for the silica of the clay pots and combines to form sodium silicate glaze over the exposed surfaces. After about ten minutes the dampers can be opened and a period of oxidation firing can follow until the kiln atmosphere is judged to be clear again (no white smoke from the chimney). This procedure is repeated a number of times whilst still raising the temperature gradually to about 1270–1280°C.

A total of about one pound of salt per cubic foot of kiln capacity will be required but the kiln bricks will also attract a salt deposit which will account for a higher salt consumption in a kiln which has not before been used for salt glazing. The salting process cannot be hurried with large doses of salt since this will result in an abrupt temperature fall; a pound or two at a time is enough but quantities should relate to kiln size. Small clay rings positioned by the spy-holes should be withdrawn from time to time as the salting operation proceeds; these should give a fairly accurate indication of the thickness of the glaze deposit. When the glaze looks thick enough, discontinue salting and, with an oxidized atmosphere, carry the temperature up to approximately 1300°C. Maintain this temperature for approximately one hour (soaking period), then switch off and seal up the kiln to ensure slow cooling.

There are two disadvantages to salt glazing:

1. Once a kiln has been used for salt glazing the residual salt deposits within the kiln will continue to affect subsequent firings for a long time afterwards. It is better to think in terms of a kiln that will be reserved for salt-glaze firings only.
2. A product of salt vapourization is hydrogen chloride—a very unhealthy atmosphere polutant to which you have a right to expose yourself, but what of others?

The qualities of good salt glazes are very pleasing so it is fortunate that alternatives are available. For example, sodium bicarbonate can be substituted for salt since it, too, will form a soda vapour. Unfortunately it is a little more difficult to use and the deposit of glaze may be rather patchy, probably due to the fact that a lower vapour pressure is produced. Oil mixed with the bicarbonate (about $\frac{1}{5}$ by volume) improves results considerably, and the dampers and secondary air vents should be closed during salting to raise the kiln pressure and hold the vapour in contact with the pots. The amount of salt deposited will depend not only on the quantities that are thrown into the firebox and how the firing is conducted; as stated previously the soda needs to combine with the silica of the clay in order to form the glaze, therefore the amount of silica available in the clay body and its particle size (fine particles are more reactive) will influence the thickness of glaze formed. Silica-rich clays develop quite thick shiny glaze deposits whereas clays with low silica content have a tendency to form irregular minute beads of glaze, like orange peel. Perhaps the simplest way to investigate this aspect of salt glazes would be to prepare a range of clay slips, some rich in and others short of silica.

These, applied to the raw pots, should enable you to judge the kind of glaze quality you prefer without involving altering the clay body. The slips could also be coloured with oxides, but be sparing because the oxides give much richer and stronger colours when used with salt glazes. Three per cent iron oxide will produce quite a dark colour.

Raw glazing

Salt glazing introduces another advantage in that the pots need only be fired once. There is no intervening biscuit firing. The dried, raw pots can be fired to glazing temperature, salted and then cooled to finish, and the economic advantages of this are obvious, especially when intermittent kilns are used. These are normally packed with raw pots, fired to biscuit temperature, cooled and unpacked; the pots are then glazed, repacked, fired to glaze maturation temperature and cooled to finish the cycle. This is a common practice which, in times of rising fuel costs, seems a close approach to folly when raw-glazing and once-firing methods can be achieved without great difficulty. It can only be assumed that it is an unfortunate legacy from industry, and, considering the particular clay bodies used, then it is an understandable one. A biscuit-fired pot is obviously much stronger than a raw pot and it will not expand, contract or soften like a raw pot when glazed.

The main consideration in raw glazing is to match the contraction of the pot with the contraction of the glaze. This can be achieved by attention to two factors:

1.	The contractability of the glaze.
2.	The contractability of the pot.

If the difference in contraction between the glaze and the pot is too great, tensions will be set up which will cause the glaze to flake off. Raw clay pots will continue to shrink after they have been raw glazed because they are still drying out. Thus they will be contracting on to interior glazes and away from exterior glazes. Glazes, on the other hand, will be contracting on to the exterior of the pots and away from the interior, so there is a reasonable prospect of compensating for one movement by means of the other. Slip glazes and glazes with a high clay content (especially of ball clays which have a higher rate of contraction) are good for raw glazing since their contraction rates will more nearly match those of the pots. Additions of bentonite can be used to raise the contraction rate of a glaze with a lower clay content. Judgement of the right moment for glazing is also important. Leather-hard pots are more resilient to moisture intake from the glaze, so the interior of a pot may be glazed whilst leather hard and the exterior when the pot is almost dry. Your judgement in these matters will be more effective as you get to know your clays and glazes better but raw glazing will certainly save you time, money and wear and tear on your kiln.

9 Choosing your kiln

It will be evident that a general path of historical development has been traced from the primitive, open-fired pre-historic method of firing pottery, to the simple up-draught Roman kiln and to the more sophisticated down draught systems which conserve heat and allow much higher temperatures to be achieved. I have intentionally encouraged an experimental approach, concentrating on the principles rather than specific examples. There is no reason to demean the simple sawdust kiln which can produce results that are unobtainable by any other means. Its characteristic qualities are demonstrated with expressive potency and sophistication by potters such as Rosemary and Denise Wren, and it may afford you appropriate means for rewarding exploration and creative expression. You may, on the other hand, be attracted to the high fired stoneware and porcelain range. If, after following these guidelines, you have acquired confidence and understanding in manipulating clay and fire, and feel sufficiently enthusiastic to contemplate some level of sustained output, then it is likely that you will feel the need for a permanent kiln, designed to accommodate the volume and type of ware produced, and which will fire reliably and economically.

Making your choice

Since the kiln is likely to represent the most costly item of expenditure for the potter and since the reliability and efficiency of the kiln is of central importance to the whole process, it is important to get the choice as nearly right as possible. In some cases you may be faced with conflicting priorities but the following considerations will have to be taken into account and choices made. Many of these points have been touched on previously, but it is useful to bring them together.

Maximum kiln operating temperature required
This will depend on the type of ware you wish to make, i.e.

> Earthenware clays and glazes—maximum temperature—1100°C approx.
> Stoneware/low temperature porcelain—maximum temperature—1300°C approx.

The higher the temperature the higher the costs.

1. Fuel consumption will be higher. The final stages of a stoneware firing (approaching 1300°C) will be consuming proportionately much more fuel than the final stages of an earthenware firing (approaching 1100°C)

2. Better (more expensive) insulating and refractory materials will be required in the kiln construction for higher temperature firings.

3. Stresses, wear and tear and deterioration of kiln structure will be more rapid at higher temperatures unless the kiln is used comfortably within its operational limits, e.g. Kanthal A.1 electric elements will have considerably shorter life when fired consistently to 1280°C–1300°C than when fired to 1250°C. Silicon carbide elements should be considered if consistently higher temperatures are required.

   Also to achieve a temperature of 1300°C may involve parts of the kiln, such as fireboxes, being subjected to considerably higher temperatures, more stress and therefore more rapid deterioration. In these situations high density firebrick must be used but ceramic fibre back-up should be incorporated to improve insulation. Insulation using ceramic fibre is dealt with in chapter 10.

Size of kiln required
This is not such an easy choice as it may initially appear to be. The choice does not simply hinge on the anticipated rate of production.

1. *Cost* As a general rule the bigger the kiln, proportionately the cheaper the firing costs, basically because with increasing size there is a diminishing surface to volume ratio and diminishing kiln structure volume to kiln chamber volume ratio. But initial building costs will be

greater for the bigger kiln and according to fuel used there may be a requirement for more powerful burners, more fuel storage capacity or 'stronger' electric elements and power supply.

2. *Convenience*   The production rate will have some influence on size of kiln required but production may be very variable. It may just be a question of personal preference whether you fire small batches of work frequently or large batches of work less frequently. Each firing however is a source of information and it is perhaps not so helpful if there is a long time lapse between making and completion, particularly if new clays, glazes or shaping and forming techniques are being explored.

3. *Siting and accommodation*   Kilns are bulky items, not readily movable, which require protective housing and appropriate ventilation. Even electric kilns emit fumes during firing and flame kilns will certainly need adequate ventilation. Fire risks must be considered. The kiln should be readily accessible with enough surrounding free space to allow heat to disperse sufficiently.

4. *Power supply*   If an electric kiln is considered it will be advisable to ensure first that the power supply is adequate. Normally the Electricity Board will not allow power rating above 7·0 kilowatts to be connected to single phase supply (equivalent to electric cooker requirements). Kilns with a 3·0 kilowatt rating or lower may be connected to a 13 amp domestic power point. Installation of three phase supply (for above 7·0 kilowatts supply) may be expensive depending upon the distance from the source of supply.

5. *Price*   When estimating what size of kiln you can afford it is important to include items such as kiln furniture, temperature indicator, heat fuse, delivery charges, VAT etc.

Choice of Fuels
This is, perhaps, the most difficult choice to make and may strongly influence all previous decisions.
The fuels traditionally used are electricity, gas (natural or bottled gas), oil and wood.

1. *Kiln atmosphere*   This choice may be made for aesthetic reasons. The means to fire under reduction conditions may be considered to be of primary importance. The colour range of glazes and clay bodies fired under reduction conditions are regarded by many potters to be much more pleasing than their oxidised counterparts. There are, however,

many potters of high repute who, by necessity or preference, are producing excellent oxidised wares.

Earthenware is usually fired under oxidising conditions and porcelain can be just as pleasing whether oxidised or reduced fired. The difference of atmosphere is most significant in the stoneware range, mainly because the reduction atmosphere enlivens the reaction of body and glaze and widens the colour range of glazes.

All fuels *can* be used in kilns to produce oxidising or reduction atmospheres but there are considerable problems and disadvantages attached to producing reduction atmospheres in electric kilns. Briefly, reduction atmospheres attack electric elements and shorten their life so seriously that it becomes prohibitively expensive. Mothballs, charcoal, natural or bottle gas will produce reduction atmospheres in electric kilns at red-hot temperatures (1000°C) and above. Silicon carbide mixed with glazes can produce localised reduction in the glaze.

Electric kiln elements made from silicon carbide rods can withstand reduction atmospheres (and much higher temperatures—1450°C) but are more expensive to install. Pots fired in saggars containing reducing agents can be used but it is not generally recommended to attempt reduction firings in electric kilns when it is so much easier and successful to reduce fire in flame fired kilns.

2. *Costs*   The cost of fuels has varied considerably in recent years. Oil, once one of the cheapest fuels, has become very much more expensive. The price of bottle gas, since it is a derivative of oil, has escalated with the price of oil. Electricity has always been comparatively expensive and still is, even when used at off-peak price. The price of natural gas has been artificially increased by the government to establish some degree of parity with other fuels. Wood, even if available locally at a reasonable price, becomes much more expensive if costing includes allowances for handling, preparation and stoking time. Waste sump oil is cheaper but presents problems of combustion, ease, and continuity of flow, and will not burn as clearly as other flame fuels.

At present, no fuel emerges with a distinct cost advantage but fuel conservation as a result of improved insulation of kilns has softened the problem of fuel costs. When costing fuels it is also necessary to consider the issues of fuel storage, burners and supplementary equipment such as compressors.

Electricity   There is no fuel storage requirement. Switch gear and power regulating systems are not excessively expensive to install and seldom require repair or replacement. The electric elements will have a variable life dependent upon use. If the elements are regularly pushed close to their limit of performance their life will be appreciably shortened. Accidental over-firing can be very expensive and some form of safety cut-out is a worthwhile consideration. Installation costs will be much higher if the supply line is not already nearby or if a three phase supply is required (for bigger kilns). It is advisable to clarify the situation with your electricity board.

Element carriers need to be carefully made to be sure that they provide efficient support and allow elements to be replaced easily when necessary. Special element carrier systems will be needed with ceramic fibre kilns unless silicon carbide elements (which are self-supporting) are used. The need for even heat distribution will determine where the elements are placed.

Gas   Bottle gas; Propane; L.P.G. (liquid petroleum gas).
This fuel is clean burning, readily accessible and adaptable. It is supplied in pressurised liquid form in cylinders. As gas is drawn from the cylinder the pressure within the cylinder drops causing the liquefied gas to boil and vaporise, so maintaining a steady supply of gas. As the vaporising gas boils it draws heat from the cylinder surface and surrounding atmosphere. If the gas is drawn off too rapidly the cylinder surface will be inadequate to allow sufficient heat transfer to vaporise the gas, the cylinder surface will frost over and gas pressure will drop. This difficulty can be overcome either by having a larger storage tank or by switching the supply between several gas cylinders. Because the gas is delivered at high pressure (15 pounds per square inch) the burners will not require the assistance of compressors or fans. The gas pressure supplied to the simple compact atmospheric burners will induce the required supply of primary air for full combustion.

Natural gas is supplied at much lower pressure and will require either large low pressure atmospheric burners or forced draught burners.

Safety precautions should be carefully observed when using gas. Bottle gas must be stored according to safety regulations and burner systems should incorporate a system which will isolate the supply in the event of flame failure. Should flame failure occur allow ample time for the evacuation of gas from the kiln interior before attempting to relight the kiln.

Oil   35 second gas oil (as used in many domestic boilers) is the most popular and readily available form. Storage is uncomplicated. According to requirement two or three 5-gallon metal drum containers could suffice or a 600 gallon storage tank for heavy users will allow advantage to be taken of lower priced bulk delivery. If the oil container can be conveniently raised to sufficient height to deliver the necessary flow by gravity feed the price of a pressure pump will be saved. Details of home-made forced draught burners are given in Chapter 8.

Wood The effects of fly ash carried into the kiln during wood firing add a characteristic quality to the ware which is favoured by many potters, but wood firing is a labour intensive activity which is not always a practical choice. Even if wood is readily available it must be stored, dried and seasoned thoroughly before use. It may take two years for green wood to dry out and season adequately. It is a bulky fuel and will require ample storage space. It will probably need to be sawn and split to the required size and certainly during the latter stages of firing the kiln will need constant regular stoking. The kiln structure will include additional provision of a fire box which represents additional building time, materials and costs.

Despite these disadvantages there are still potters who prize the qualities obtained by wood firing sufficiently to dedicate themselves to the labours involved and feel that their efforts are well rewarded.

10 Kiln design developments using ceramic fibre

An efficient kiln, which can perform satisfactorily and reliably is of central importance to the potter, and it is in the sphere of kiln structure and performance that quite dramatic changes have taken place recently. The changes have been made possible by the development of vastly superior insulating materials, which may be used to counteract the striking escalation of fuel and energy costs. The changes have been directed towards (a) much faster firing cycles—made possible by improved thermal efficiency and thermal shock resistance of the improved insulation materials (b) light-weight kiln constructions, as the new materials are low in density and (c) ease and speed of kiln construction, as the materials are simple to install.

Ceramic fibre

The 'new' ceramic fibre insulating material has been available for about twenty-five years, although until recently it has been used largely in industry. Perhaps it required the escalating cost of energy to stimulate studio potters' interest in this material, but today there are few commercially produced small studio kilns being marketed which are not constructed predominantly or in part with ceramic fibre insulation.

Advantages of ceramic fibre

Ceramic fibre linings are 75% lighter than insulating fibrebrick linings, and 90–95% lighter than dense refractory linings. Because heat storage is directly proportional to the density of material used in a furnace lining, considerably less heat energy is required to bring the light-weight ceramic fibre-lined kiln up to maximum temperature. Cooling can also be quicker without risk of thermal shock to the kiln lining and therefore firing cycles can be shorter. Because ceramic fibre linings are more thermally efficient a thinner lining can be used with a gain in kiln capacity. Fibre linings are resilient and will withstand movement without cracking. Ceramic blankets and papers can easily be cut with scissors or knives, boards can be sawn easily and installation is both quick and easy compared with traditional brick linings. Supporting structures can be much lighter since the weight loadings are so much lower.

Ceramic fibre products are significantly more expensive than traditional insulating or refractory linings but 20–40% fuel savings can be realistically anticipated which will compensate for the initial extra cost. Another important advantage is that ceramic fibre kilns can be designed for disassembly and portability if necessary. I still regret losing more than £1000 worth of high grade insulation bricks when I dismantled my kiln. The jointing compound had hardened with firing and the bricks broke in every direction other than along the jointing seams. They were fit only to use as an insulating aggregate for a subsequent building project.

The advantages of using ceramic fibre insulation may be summarised as follows:

Low heat storage
Low thermal conductivity } Fuel economy
High heat reflectance } Shorter firing cycles

Thermal shock resistance
Excellent chemical and thermal } Long-term working
    stability } efficiency of kiln

Light-weight, easily } Ease and simplicity of
    manipulated material } construction/repair

Properties of ceramic fibre

Ceramic fibre is produced by melting essentially pure alumina and silica together at extremely high temperatures. This molten material is poured past strong air jets which blow the melt into very fine strands which cool and harden. This 'fibre' is then made up into various marketable forms which include bulk fibre, blanket, board, paper and an extensive variety of vacuum-shaped forms.

Ceramic fibre is an efficient insulating material because of the low heat conductivity of the component elements, and its low thermal mass. It is

117

Figs. 77 and 78 Ceramic fibre is marketed in a wide variety of forms, including paper, board, yarn, cloth and vacuum formed sections, but the most suitable for general kiln building purposes is the blanket form which is available in varying thickness, densities, and thermal insulation qualities. (Courtesy of the Carborundum Company Ltd)

very light, because the open texture of fibres contain a high proportion of air spaces and still air is a very poor conductor of heat. Basically, the factors which affect the performance of ceramic fibre are the chemical composition of the different 'grades' of the material, the different manufacturing processes used, and shrinkage which occurs at high temperatures.

Chemical composition

Where the ratio of alumina to silica is higher the melting point will be higher—for example:

(a) 62% alumina : 38% silica—melting point 1928°C—continuous use limit 1427°C

(b) 48% alumina : 51·8% silica—melting point 1790°C—continuous use limit 1260°C

Where additional chemicals are introduced for specific functions they may also affect thermal properties, as in (c):

(c) 37–43% alumina : 55–60% silica; calcium oxide 7·5%: titanium oxide 1·7%—melting point 1648°C—continuous use limit 927°C

Manufacture of ceramic fibre

Fibre length and diameter vary according to the manufacturing process and chemical composition. Long staple fibres are generally more resistant to breakdown from mechanical stress and vibration. Manufacturing processes (e.g. washing) which remove unfiberised particles, result in clean and more thermally efficient products. The way in which the fibres are 'woven' or 'felted' together (cross-locked and needled) will also affect handling properties.

Shrinkage

The main problem when using ceramic fibre is the low but still significant shrinkage (known as 'irreversible linear change') which occurs when heating to high temperatures. This shrinkage, which may, for example, average approximately 4·5% with sustained regular use at 1260°C, is irreversible. The manufacturer's recommended maximum working temperature is determined by the level of shrinkage—not the melting point, which is usually considerably higher. Unless this is borne in mind and catered for when ceramic fibre is used there could be quite serious loss of insulation.

Some ceramic fibre products are treated (with chrome for example) to reduce shrinkage which allows the product to be used at higher temperatures. Another way to limit the shrinkage problem is to buy pre-fired and therefore pre-shrunk materials, but this is usually prohibitively expensive.

Kiln construction using ceramic fibre

The ceramic fibre preparation most suitable to the studio potter for kiln construction is the blanket or felt form. Assuming a required maximum working temperature of 1350°C, there are principally two different methods of physically applying this material which may be used.

1. The fibre blanket may be layered, using appropriate thicknesses of suitable grades of blanket, and secured by ceramic studs and washers. (For kilns designed to operate at temperatures up to 1150°C with oxidising atmospheres Inconel 601 or stainless steel 310 studs with ceramic cuplocks can be used.) Suppliers will advise on grades and thicknesses of blanket to be used according to the required performance of a particular kiln. The main advantage of this system is that successive blanket layers may be selected for appropriate quality and thickness according to the temperature gradient between hot and cold faces of the kiln wall. Expensive high grade hot face blanket can be used conservatively with appropriate lower grade and cheaper back-up layers.

   When kiln operating temperatures exceed 1150°C the hot face shingle layering system should be used and at all time joints in

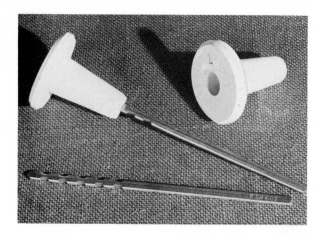

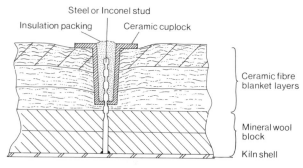

Fig. 80 Cuplock and stud securing system for ceramic fibre blanket layers (line illustration).

Steel or Inconel stud

Insulation packing   Ceramic cuplock

Ceramic fibre blanket layers

Mineral wool block

Kiln shell

Fig. 79 Cuplocks and studs for securing layered ceramic blanket linings. Stainless steel or Inconel 601 studs of appropriate length are welded, screwed, bolted or cemented to the kiln wall. The layers of ceramic blanket of suitable grade and thickness are impaled on the studs and held in position by the ceramic cuplocks which are locked to the stud ends. Manufacturers' specifications for grade and thickness of blanket, method of layering and studding patterns for required operational temperatures should be followed implicitly.

(Courtesy of the Carborundum Company Ltd)

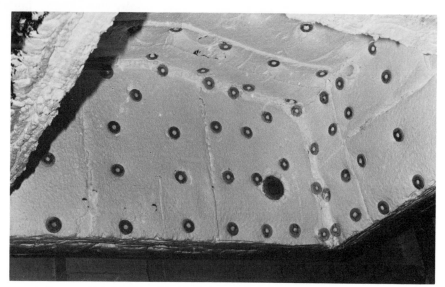

Fig. 81 View looking upwards into Clive Davies' 'top-hat' kiln. The lightweight ceramic fibre blanket lining, secured by ceramic cuplocks on studs, makes the top-hat kiln a viable proposition for the studio potter.

adjacent blanket layers should be staggered. The main disadvantage is that the securing system of pegs is not an easy do-it-yourself operation without the necessary equipment.

2. Although compressed, edge-folded blanket modules can be purchased ready made, they are much cheaper to make from a suitable grade of ceramic blanket. They consist of 12 inch strips of blanket folded in half along the length to produce a width the same as the thickness required to line the kiln. A series of these strips are laid side by side in a 12 inch wide wooden jig, and then compressed into a 12 × 12 inch module. The module can be held in compression by string, scrim, plastic netting, etc.

120

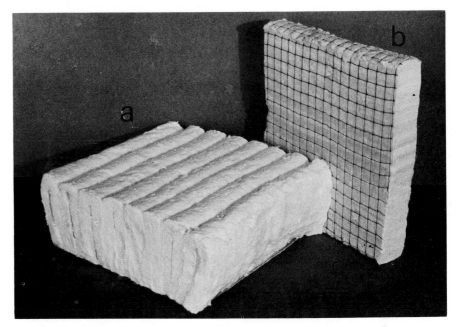

until secured in the kiln wall. The folded edges comprise the module hot face, which at high temperatures will tighten up when shrinkage occurs and prevent gaps forming.

Suppliers will advise on the grade of blanket to be used and the thickness of the module. The modules should be arranged in rows, all facing the same way. The rows should be separated by folded batten strips compressed firmly between the cut edges of the modules (see Figs. 83 and 84).

The modules should be attached to the outer casing with a refractory adhesive. A suitable outer kiln casing would be heavy gauge expanded wire, which would provide a good key for the adhesive. The material holding the module in compression can be left in position since it will fire out with the first firing. Edge folded batten strips compressed into corners and wall to roof joints will take care of contraction which may occur at these points.

The advantage of this method is that, although it may take more time to cut and form the modules, all stages of the process can be achieved with simple basic equipment and a little care. It will however, be necessary to construct the module entirely from one grade of blanket which will meet the hot face performance requirement (as opposed to the layer blanket method above). Because of this it will prove a somewhat more expensive method.

121

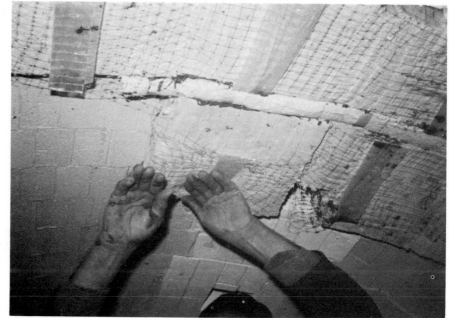

Fig. 83   A lining of edge-stacked ceramic fibre modules being applied with cement directly onto the interior refractory roof arch to improve insulation. Note the plastic netting which retains the module shape and compression during application. Note also the edge-folded batten strips applied between the rows of modules to eliminate contraction gaps. (Courtesy of Carborundum Company Ltd)

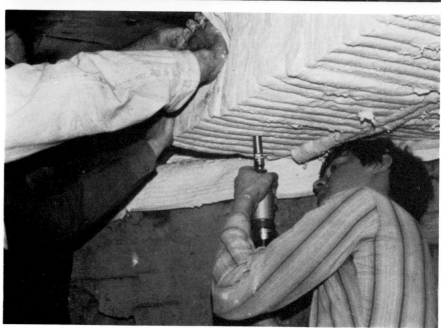

Fig. 84   Manufactured edge-folded ceramic fibre anchored modules, cemented to expanded metal backing, being held under compression and attached to the kiln roof with self-tapping anchor screws. Note the edge-folded batten strip applied between the rows of modules to eliminate shrinkage gaps. (Courtesy of the Carborundum Company Ltd.)

122

Fig. 85 Interior view of Norman Darby's Saffil module lined kiln. This is a catenary arch, wood and oil fired kiln which shows no attack from fly ash. Note the chequer arrangement of the edge-stacked modules which are secured with refractory cement to an outer skin of fire brick. Saffil, an ICI product, is comprised of almost pure alumina ceramic fibre. Shrinkage problems are minimal and therefore the chequer pattern of application is appropriate to this product—but it is a considerably more expensive material.

The manufacturers will advise not only what grade of blanket and thickness of module is necessary but also what the compressive density of the module should be (this question is discussed in more detail below). The ceramic fibre blanket is manufactured to a range of pre-determined and specified compressive densities, e.g. 4 lb, 6 lb, and 8 lb per cubic foot, so it would be very simple to calculate how many strips per module of a specified weight and thickness of blanket would be required to achieve the density and thickness you want. If it is necessary to confirm calculations the module need only be weighed on the kitchen scales!

Example: Using a 2 inch blanket of 4 lb cubic ft. density, it will require six 12 × 12 inch slabs edge folded and compressed to produce a 12 × 12 × 6 inch module of 8 lb cubic ft compressive density.

The effect of compression on the insulating properties of ceramic fibre

The excellent insulating properties of ceramic products are due to:

(a) The low thermal conductivity of ceramic fibre.
(b) The low conductivity of still air trapped between the ceramic fibre threads.
(c) The low density of ceramic fibre which limits heat storage.

123

Within certain limits the insulating properties of ceramic blanket improve with compression but above 25 lb per cubic foot the insulating benefit of trapped air is seriously diminished and the increased compressive density of the blanket produces an unacceptable increase in heat storage. The more usual working range for ceramic blanket is between 4 lb per cubic foot and 8 lb per cubic foot.
For example:

Compressive density	Thickness of edge-folded blanket	Hot face temp	Cold face temp
7 lb/ft³	6 inches	1316°C	132°C
8 lb/ft³	6 inches	1316°C	118°C

Thickness of ceramic fibre walls

A low cold face temperature would seem to indicate that the heat was being effectively contained within the kiln. Unfortunately, this is not necessarily true since the thickness of kiln wall, however good its insulating properties, still represents a thermal mass capable of absorbing and storing heat and the thicker the wall, the more heat it will store. In fact, a point of balance occurs when further increase of wall thickness *reduces* thermal efficiency because proportionately more heat is being stored in the thermal mass of the wall structure than would be lost to the atmosphere from a thinner wall.
For example:

Compressive density	Thickness of edge-folded blanket	Hot face temp	Cold face temp
8 lb/ft³	3 inches	1316°C	118°C
8 lb/ft³	10 inches	1316°C	89°C

For the addition of more than three times the thickness of insulating ceramic fibre wall, the fall in cold face temperature is only 29°C. Although it is necessary to achieve an acceptable cold face working temperature this must be viewed in relation to the additional cost of extra ceramic fibre used and extra heat energy lost to heat storage in the kiln wall.

Yet another problem arises with layered wall constructions. Whilst it is easy to understand that materials commonly used in kiln building have varied properties of insulation dependent upon their density, thermal conductivity and thickness, it may be less obvious that these values are changed by the addition of back-up insulation. For example, the temperature gradient between the hot face and cold face of, say, a standard firebrick is quite considerably lowered by the addition of even a very thin layer (1–2 mm) of ceramic fibre paper; i.e. the brick cold face becomes *hotter* because the heat is being held back within the brick. The *heat storage* of the firebrick is being increased. Whilst the cold face of the ceramic fibre paper is lower in temperature than the former cold face of the firebrick, more heat is actually being stored in the firebrick itself.

This all makes it very difficult for the do-it-yourself kiln builder to predict with any degree of certainty precisely what thicknesses, grades and forms of refractory and insulating materials will be most efficient and economical to use. Fortunately, the manufacturers and suppliers of these materials are anxious to help and will readily give advice when consulted. In order to help, the supplier will need to have the following information:

(a) Peak operating temperature
(b) Desired cold face temperature
(c) Optimum heat loss data
(d) Gas velocity inside the kiln
(e) Furnace atmosphere and type of fuel

The supplier's recommendations will be determined by computer programme which will take account of:

(a) Hot face temperature
(b) Ambient temperature
(c) Thermal conductivities of material of construction
(d) Thickness of each material
(e) Heat given off by kiln casing
(f) Outside air flow

Probably a range of alternative wall constructions will be recommended.

Abrasion

Ceramic fibre is not very resistant to abrasion. Layered blanket linings are more susceptible to damage than compressed module linings, but with careful use and thoughtful design this is not a serious problem.

An alternative way of attaching ceramic fibre which removes the risk of damage by abrasion to the interior fibre lining is the Shelley Fibre Sandwich Construction System. This allows for a thin kiln lining of dense refractory tiles over the appropriately layered ceramic fibre lining. The tiles are secured by lock-in refractory tie bars attached to stainless steel sockets welded on mild steel bars secured to the kiln casing. Not only is this system useful to protect the fibre lining from mechanical

Flat roof and wall construction without elements (for flame kilns)

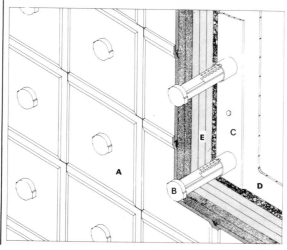

Side wall construction with coil elements (for electric kilns)

Fig. 86 *The Shelley Fibre Sandwich Construction System*

This system provides a thin lining of dense, abrasive, resistant refractory tiles over the appropriate layers of ceramic fibre lining. The tiles are available with:
1. *Overlapping joints for flame kilns*
or
2. *Butt joints and elements troughs for electric kilns.*
The tiles (A) are held by lock-in refractory tie-bars (B), attached to steel sockets welded on mild steel bars (C), secured to the kiln casing (D), sandwiching the ceramic fibre (E). Electric element trough is F.
(Courtesy of Donald Shelley Ltd)

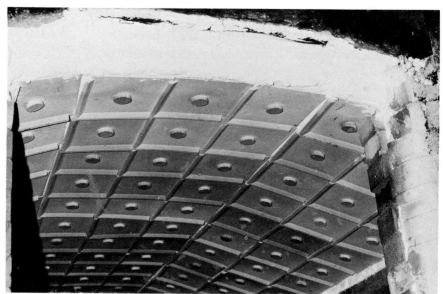

Fig. 87 *Interior view of Colin Kellam's oil-fired kiln, constructed mainly in firebrick, but the roof arch is lined with ceramic fibre blanket faced with edge-lapped refractory tiles on the Shelley fibre sandwich principle.*

damage but it would also be an asset where products of combustion such as sulphur dioxide or fly ash (high alkali) might cause deterioration of the fibre lining. It would also afford protection in parts of the kiln lining exposed to high velocity gases. The installation costs would be considerably higher but in certain circumstances this could be justified.

126

Fig. 88 A typical example of the new breed of portable studio electric kilns. The light-weight, high quality insulation brick lining is backed with ceramic fibre. The lid is also constructed from ceramic fibre which provides excellent insulation and ease of operation. (Courtesy of Kilns and Furnaces Ltd)

Alternative ways of using ceramic fibre in kiln construction

If you are not fully convinced of the benefits of ceramic fibre kiln constructions there are alternatives which could be considered. Ceramic fibre can be used to advantage as an interior lining over refractory walls or as a back-up material. This way of using it has become particularly popular with the introduction of new light-weight insulation brick, manufactured in the United States by Babcock and Wilcox and marketed in England by Ray Scott of Fordham Thermal Systems Co Ltd, under the name of SAYVIT bricks.

The brick is of standard size, $9 \times 4\frac{1}{2} \times 3$ inches, weighing 50% less than conventional high temperature insulation (HTI) bricks and has

127

very low thermal conductivity rating, low permanent linear shrinkage, and a working temperature of 1300°C.

Many commercially produced small electric studio kilns designed to operate at up to 1300°C are now using an inner 3–4 inch lining of this new low thermal mass firebrick, backed by a thin layer (approximately ½–1 inch) of lower grade ceramic fibre blanket and cased in thin metal sheet. The standard top-loading lids for these kilns are often formed from 3–4 inch deep strips of high grade ceramic fibre blanket compress packed on edge. This provides a light-weight lid structure which is much easier to hinge and operate. Frequently these kilns are now constructed as a cylinder or oval for speed and economy of assembly, with light-weight metal pot-riveted outer casings.

The only disadvantage of this excellent insulating brick is its low crushing strength. It should be handled with care to avoid breakage. Wherever possible I would recommend dry brick assembly. Refractory and insulation bricks are usually produced to precise dimensions with smooth, well-finished surfaces and ceramic fibre paper may be used for insulation 'gaskets' between the bricks if necessary. Firebox linings and bag walls particularly may want adjustment or replacement from time to time and this is a much easier proposition if dry brick installation has been employed. If the sideways thrust of an arch is contained by the support framework, then even the arch may be constructed dry since it will be self-locking and self-supporting.

Some thoughts and comments in conclusion

Those who have been stimulated into activity by the preceding chapters will soon be sharing experiences similar to those of the learner driver—'Which gear am I in now?' 'Where *has* the clutch pedal gone?' 'I didn't really want to light a cigarette—I thought it was the starter!' Your fingers will be all thumbs, and the clay will have a will of its own—one which is opposite to yours! Even the simplest operations will be bedevilled by the worst 'bad luck'. But this is another form of fire which the would-be potter must pass through—the fire of initiation—and there is no way to escape it! In time the learner driver ceases to be a raw learner; it is impossible to define the exact moment when this happens but he will suddenly realize that he has made a beautifully sweet gear change without even thinking about it. Later on the mechanics of driving become almost a series of reflexes and the driver can concentrate on the advanced skills, relating to other road users and conditions. Thus he builds a fund of driving experience while at the same time improving his anticipation. These are skills which will develop continuously in the future.

Sheer mastery of the skills of pottery is not the ultimate objective. The skills are only important in as much that they make it possible to manipulate the materials in an appropriate manner. But 'the appropriate manner' is very much the product of a sympathetic feeling for the materials and their potential. It is not good enough to beat the clay into submission; a harmony between the artist/craftsman and his materials is essential. Moreover, the skill is neither in the fingertips nor in the arm muscles but in the mind which is able, in a reasoning way, to establish understanding through experience. The fingers and eyes are the sensory receptors for tactile and visual experience. Discovery, enquiry, invention and imagination are mental processes; the creative concept, by definition, is formed in the mind.

Although the manipulative skills may be inadequate to allow the creative concept to materialize in the intended image, the act of making is itself an enriching experience which will in some measure condition subsequent responses. As Giacommetti said, 'My failures interest me as much as my successes.' Unless you are prepared to make failures you will make nothing.

The powers of imagination, enquiry, discovery and invention need at least as much exercising as the fingers and arm muscles, and the development which will subsequently take place will have a general rather than specific application which will not merely feed back in a narrow way into your area of interest in pottery but will contribute to your development and awareness in general. Conversely, your experiences and discoveries during day-to-day life will feed back at conscious and subconscious levels into your pottery work, and this is both right and good since pottery is not developed in a vacuum as an isolated activity and will thrive only if you have breadth and depth of all kinds of experience to draw upon. When it comes to making your statement you will need something interesting to say. Some people struggle with determination to be original or to make something different—not that the two are synonymous—but the 'originality' dilemma usually arises when the 'cart is placed before the horse'. Originality cannot be conjured up at that moment when you sit down at the table with an enticing lump of freshly wedged clay. It begins when you are waiting for the bus at the stop by the builder's yard and become fascinated by the way in which the light falling on a stack of drainpipes produces an exciting relief, it begins as you peel the mushrooms for supper or as you stop to look at the stones and wood wedged in the eroded breakwater you have just clambered over. Fortunately we are not all equally excited by the same visual experiences so it is here that originality begins, and the effort to be original would be more profitably directed in exercising visual awareness. When you have feasted visually and digested your experiences originality will be far more likely to distinguish your work because it will be inspired by personal and individual discoveries. Clay and the traditions of pottery are ubiquitous—but you are unique!

Many are called but few are chosen to become the leading potters of tomorrow, nor is it the intention of this book to set the reader on the path to pottery success—whatever that may be! The pressures of achievement may hinder the enjoyment of this experience; or there may evolve a tendency to play safe and shelter within the security of the tried and proven formulas for results, but such results have their own price. Working with clay and fire can be an enjoyment and education in itself, drawing on the resources of imagination, invention and discovery; it involves experiencing failures but these make its successes the sweeter.

130

Appendix: temperature-colour guide

Temperature—Colour guide

0–470°C	No visible colour
470–550°C	First visible colour—very dark red
550–650°C	Dark cherry red Approx. seger cone 021 Approx. orton cone 020
650–800°C	Cherry red to bright cherry Approx. seger cone 021--014 Approx. orton cone 020–015
800–900°C	Bright cherry to orange-red Approx. seger cone 014–010 Approx. orton cone 015–011
900–1050°C	Orange-red to orange-yellow Approx. seger cone 010–03 Approx. orton cone 011–05
1050–1200°C	Orange-yellow to straw yellow Approx. seger cone 03–6 Approx. orton cone 05–4
1200–1300°C	Straw yellow to yellow-white Approx. seger cone 6–10 Approx. orton cone 4–9

As temperature progresses from the first visible dark red glow so the colour spectrum changes through red to yellow and to almost white at 1300°C. In the absence of either pyrometric cones or a pyrometer it is possible to determine if a glaze has melted by inserting a cold metal rod through the spy-hole (only with current off in the case of an electric kiln). If the rod is held near a pot inside it will be seen reflected on the glaze surface if the glaze is mature. Small glazed rings accessible through the spy-hole can also be drawn out on a metal hook to verify the progression of the firing, but seger or orton pyrometric cones are cheap, reliable and preferable for accurate results. It is advisable to keep an accurate record of each firing including prevailing weather conditions, type of firing (biscuit or glazed), and type and quantity of fuel used; and a progressive record of temperature (estimated or measured) and adjustments to controls (dampers, burners etc.). With experience you will be better able to predict firing progress and obtain greater efficiency from your kiln.

Reduction

During reduction firings the smoky interior atmosphere of the kiln will slightly dull the colour of the fire. Smoke and flame pouring from the chimney is not the best indicator of a reducing atmosphere. Reduction is best indicated by the positive pressure within the kiln; when the spy-hole bung is

Fig. 88 Some sample firing schedules. There are almost as many different firing schedules as there are potters. These graphs give only a general indication of the differences between various kinds of firings. There are so many contributing factors such as weather, packing, fuel regulation etc., which influence results to such an extent that each firing is another opportunity for further discovery

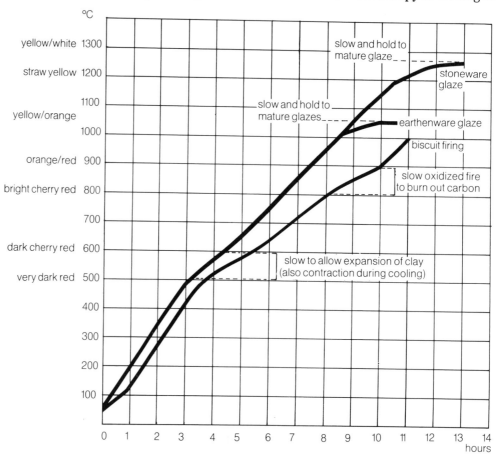

removed flame will issue at first but may die back since the removal of the bung may be sufficient to release the positive pressure. Reduction may be harmful before 900°C; it is normally started at approximately 1000°C so that the clay body is affected before the glazes melt and seal over the surface. Excessive reduction may cool the kiln. Alternating oxidizing and reducing atmospheres are often used but this is to some extent personal preference and must be judged by the results.

Glaze ingredient analysis graphs
Fluxes (F), alumina (A), silica (S)

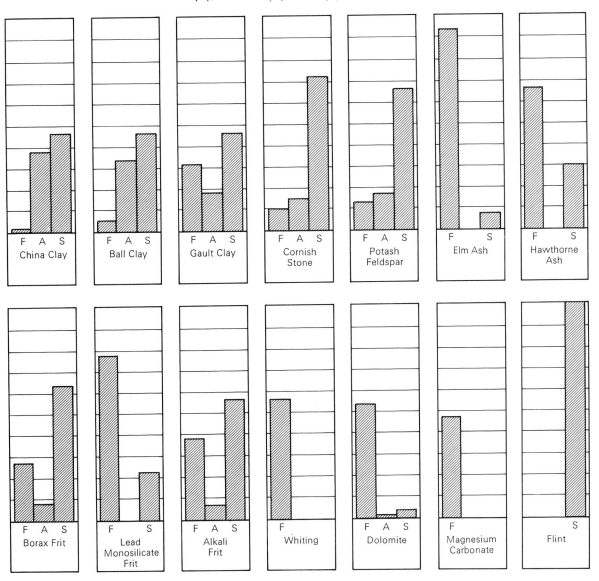

Materials and equipment

Suppliers

General suppliers of most pottery equipment and materials:

Ferro (Great Britain) Ltd, Wombourne, Wolverhampton WV5 8DA, Tel. 0902 894144.

The Fulham Pottery Ltd, Burlington House, 184 New Kings' Road, London SW6 4PB, Tel. 01 731 2167.

Potclays Ltd, Brickkiln Lane, Etruria, Stoke-on-Trent, Staffs. ST4 7BP, Tel. 0782 29816.

Pottery Crafts Ltd, Campbell Road, Stoke-on-Trent, Staffs. ST4 4ET, Tel. 0782 272444 (formerly Wengers, Podmores and Harrison Mayers).

Clays

Moira Pottery Co. Ltd, Moira, Burton-upon-Trent, Staffs. DE12 6DF, Tel. 0283 221961.

Mellor Clays, Etruria Vale, Stoke-on-Trent, Staffs. ST1 4DD, Tel. 0782 23441.

Kiln Furniture

Acme Marls Ltd, Clough St, Hanley, Stoke-on-Trent, Staffs. Tel. 0782 260848.

Electric Kiln Elements

Labheat, Ironbridge, Staffs. Tel. 095 245 3158.

Litherlands' Elements Ltd, Navigations Rd, Burslem, Stoke-on-Trent, Staffs. Tel. 0782 814 024.

Hall and Pickles, Manchester 1.

Refractory cement (ciment fondu)
Lafarge Aluminous Cement Co. Ltd, 73 Brook St, London W1.

Castable Refractories
G.R. Stein Refractories Ltd, Monolithics Division, Station Rd, Deepcar, Sheffield.

Refractory and insulation bricks
'Sayvit' 1300 refractory bricks, Fordham Thermal Systems, 37 Midenhall Rd, Fordham, Ely, Cambs. CB7 5NW.
Gibbons Refractories Ltd, PO Box 19, Dudley, W. Midlands, Tel. 0384 53251.
M.P.K. Insulation Ltd, Hythe Works, Colchester, Essex.

Ceramic Fibre
The Carborundum Company Ltd, Mill Lane, Rainford, St Helens, Merseyside WA11 8LP, Tel. 074 488 2941.
Morganite Ceramic Fibre Ltd, Tebay Rd, Bromborough, Wirrall, Merseyside, Tel. 051 3344 030.
'Saffil' Marketing Dept, ICI Ltd, Mond Division, The Heath, Runcorn, Cheshire WA7 4QS, Tel. 09285 78221.
Donald Shelley Ltd (Fibre sandwich construction system), Mount Industrial Estate, Stone, Staffs. Tel. 0785 812313.

Electric Kilns
British Ceramic Service Co. Ltd, Bricesco House, Park Avenue, Wolstanton, Newcastle, Staffs. ST5 8AT, Tel. 0782 626 204.
Catterson-Smith, Woodrolfe Rd, Tollesbury, near Maldon, Essex CM9 8SJ, Tel. 062 186 342.
Cromartie Kilns Ltd, Parkhall Rd, Longton, Stoke-on-Trent, Staffs. ST3 5AY, Tel. 0782 313 947.
Kilns and Furnaces Ltd, Keele St, Tunstall, Stoke-on-Trent, Staffs. ST6 5AS, Tel. 0782 813621.

Colouring oxides:
Blythe Colour Works, Creswell, Stoke-on-Trent.

Delivery charges will add considerably to costs so wherever possible explore local resources. Firebricks and refractory cements, for example, will probably be stocked by local builders' merchants.

Fig. 63—List of components and suppliers

Four 17-inch Dexian angle irons (upright corners allowing $3\frac{1}{4}$-inch leg).

Six $18\frac{1}{2}$-inch Dexian angle irons (floor corners and floor-centre supports).

Two 9-inch Dexian angle irons (lid hinge filament).

Four $18\frac{1}{2}$-inch Dexian straps (frame-top ties).

Two 27-inch Dexian straps (lid ties).

Six $20 \times \frac{3}{8}$ inch mild steel rods, 1 inch threaded at each end (lid ties, hinge and handle).

Twelve nuts and washers to fit the $\frac{3}{8}$-inch rod.

One connection box approx. $6 \times 6 \times 3$ inches (control-box housing).

Two arcolectric neon indicator lights, $\frac{1}{4}$ watt.

Two porcelain connectors.

Heavy-duty, asbestos-covered copper wire; 2 feet should be enough.

A suitable length of flexible 13-amp cable.

One 3-kW Kanthal A1 element; available from Litherland's Elements Ltd, Navigation Rd, Burslem, Stoke-on-Trent, Staffordshire.

One Sunvic energy regulator, type TYX/PI; available from Associated Electrical Industries Ltd, Instrument Division, Domestic and Industrial Components Dept, PO Box 1, Harlow, Essex.

Forty-three $9 \times 4\frac{1}{2} \times 3$ inch, high temperature insulating bricks; available from Kingscliffe Insulating Products Ltd, (KIP 26 Bricks) Storrs Bridge Works, Loxley, Nr Sheffield *or* Gibbons (Dudley) Ltd, (HT1 Bricks) Dibdale Works, Nr Dudley, Worcestershire *or* SAYVIT bricks (see above for supplier)

Four $18\frac{1}{4} \times 13\frac{1}{2} \times \frac{1}{4}$ inch Fiberfrax sheets (sides).

One $18\frac{1}{4} \times 18\frac{1}{2} \times \frac{1}{4}$ inch Fiberfrax sheet (base).

One $9 \times 13\frac{3}{4} \times \frac{1}{4}$ inch Fiberfrax sheet (control-box backing).

} Carborundum Company Ltd.

Basic requirements

1 sieve frame and clip, 10-inch diameter.

Phosphor-bronze mesh for 10-inch frame, 80-mesh.

Note: The above are the component parts for one pottery sieve.

1 cup lawn $2\frac{3}{4}$-inch diameter plastic frame, 100-mesh.

1 1-pint mortar with pestle.

1 set of plastic measuring spoons.

1 medium-size, hard rubber kidney palette.

1 medium-size, extra-flexible steel kidney scraper.

Note: The above will have to be purchased but the articles below can probably be borrowed from the kitchen or obtained from local sources at little or no cost.

1 pair of long-handled iron tongs.

Plastic mixing bowls and buckets with lids for clay, slips and glazes.

Decorators' plastic paint containers. These are extremely useful; you can't
  have too many.
1 wooden rolling-pin, approximately $1\frac{3}{4}$-inch diameter. Alternatively, lengths
  of wood can be bought from timber merchants; shaped handles can get in
  the way.
Cutting wire.
2 or 3 synthetic sponges; offcuts or packing pieces will do.
1 small piece of chamois leather for smoothing damp clay edges.
Some thin slats of wood (approximately 18 inch long) for rolling guides.
Plastic sheeting for covering work and wrapping clay.
Cloth—old sheeting, onion sacks, etc. on which to roll out clay.
A collection of knives, forks and spoons for various purposes, other than
  eating.
Plastic detergent bottles for slip trailing and making combs.
1 packet of paper hand-towels to prevent the clay sticking to formers.
1 nail brush for sieving.
An assortment of brushes: thick, thin, soft, stiff, large and small for
  decorating.
1 small garden hand spray for applying glazes, slips and oxides.
Scales.

No doubt you will find that you need many other small items, such as pen
caps and nails for cutting and making holes; most of these you will be able to
find around the home.

Glaze ingredients

Potash feldspar	14 lb	Lead bisilicate	
Cornish stone	14 lb	Frit	7 lb
Whiting	14 lb	Borax frit	7 lb
Flint	14 lb	Alkali frit	7 lb
China clay (powdered)	14 lb	Cobalt oxide	$\frac{1}{4}$ lb
Ball clay (powdered)	14 lb	Manganese oxide	$\frac{1}{2}$ lb
Dolomite	7 lb	Red iron oxide	2 lb
Magnesium carbonate	3 lb	Black copper oxide	$\frac{1}{2}$ lb
Bentonite	4 lb		

Recommended books

The Energy Efficient Potter Regis C. Brodie (Watson Guptill).
Pioneer Pottery Michael Cardew (Longman)
Electric Kiln Pottery Emmanuel Cooper (Batsford).
Electric Kiln Construction for Potters Robert Fournier (Van Nostrand Reinhold).
The Self-Reliant Potter Andrew Holden (A & C Black).
The Kiln Book Frederick Olsen (Chilton).
Ceramic Glazes Cullen W. Parmelee (Cahners).
Clays and Glazes for the Potter Daniel Rhodes (A & C Black).
Ceramic Skillbooks series (A & C Black).
Clays Frank and Janet Hamer.
Saltglaze Peter Starkey.
Pottery Science Martin Wickham.
Oriental Glazes Nigel Wood.
The Technique of Pottery Dora Billington (Batsford).
Glazes for the Craft Potter Harry Frazer (A & C Black).
Understanding Pottery Glazes David Green (Faber & Faber).
A Potter's Book Bernard Leach (Faber & Faber).
Clay and Glazes for the Potter Daniel Rhodes (A & C Black).
Kilns: Design, Construction and Operation Daniel Rhodes (A & C Black).

Index